Better Homes and Gardens®
Hearts & Flowers Cross-Stitch

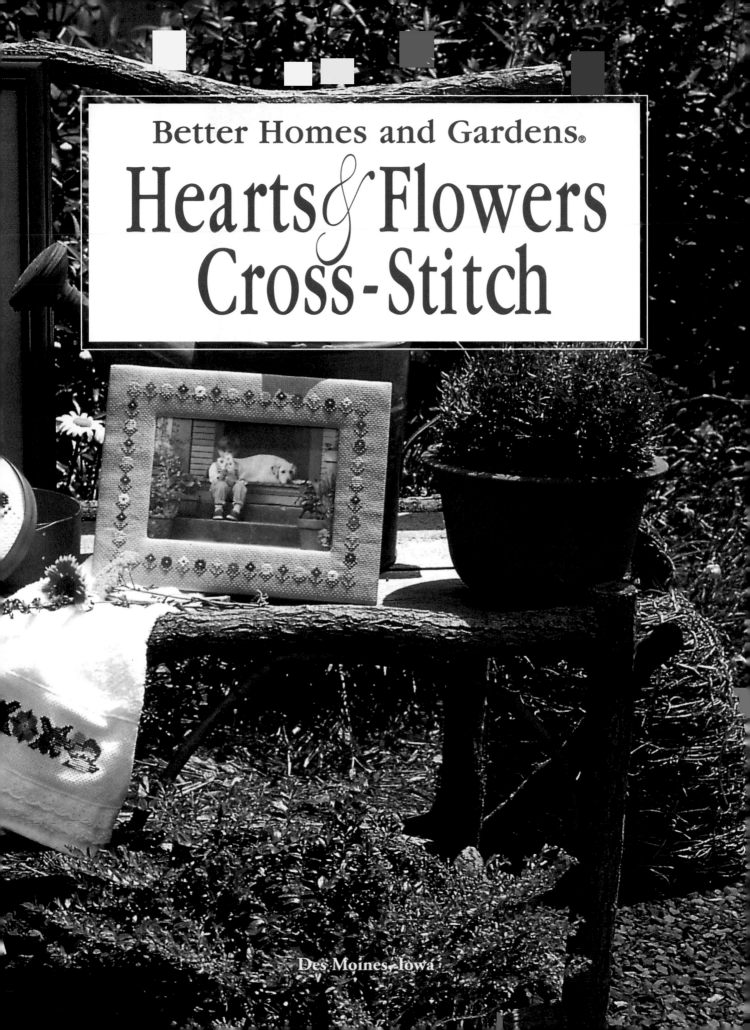

Better Homes and Gardens®
Hearts & Flowers Cross-Stitch

Des Moines, Iowa

Better Homes and Gardens® Books
An imprint of Meredith® Books

Hearts & Flowers Cross-Stitch

Senior Editor: *Carol Spier*
Assistant Editor: *Bonita Eckhaus*
Associate Art Director: *Lynda Haupert*
Production Manager: *Bill Rose*
Creative Editor: *Karin Strom*
Photography: *Julie Maris Semel*
Charts and Illustrations: *Phoebe Adams Gaughan*
Technical Editors: *Barbara Fimbel, Susanna Pfeffer,*
Barbara Sestok
Electronic Production Coordinator: *Paula Forest*
♥
Vice President, Editorial Director: *Elizabeth P. Rice*
Executive Editor: *Maryanne Bannon*
Art Director: *Ernest Shelton*
Managing Editor: *Christopher Cavanaugh*
♥
President, Book Group: *Joseph J. Ward*
Vice President, Retail Marketing: *Jamie L. Martin*
Vice President, Direct Marketing: *Timothy Jarrell*

Meredith Corporation

Chairman of the Executive Committee:
E.T. Meredith III
Chairman of the Board and Chief Executive Officer:
Jack D. Rehm
President and Chief Operating Officer:
William T. Kerr

ISBN: 0-696-00064-4 (hardcover)
ISBN: 0-696-20435-5 (softcover)
Library of Congress Catalog Card Number: 93-080859

Printed in the United States of America
10 9 8 7 6 5 4 3 2 1

WE CARE!

All of us at Better Homes and Gardens® Books
are dedicated to offering you, our customer, the best
books we can create. We are particularly concerned
that all of our instructions for making projects are clear
and accurate. Please address your correspondence to
Customer Service, Meredith Press,
150 East 52nd Street, New York, NY 10022.

If you would like to order additional copies of
any of our books, call 1-800-678-8901 or check
with your local bookstore.

For centuries stitchers have turned to the garden for inspiration. Textiles adorned with floral motifs remain from as far back as the days of the Pharaohs of ancient Egypt. And flowers have been associated with romance since time immemorial. From a lovers' stroll along a garden path to the sentimental gesture of sending a dozen roses, flowers seem to open everyone's heart.

♥

What better theme, then, for a cross-stitch book than Hearts and Flowers? Hearts and flowers offer an endless variety of colors and motifs—the palette is a virtual rainbow and there are countless species of flowers to choose from. The heart shape is universal, a perfect complement to any flower design. Because the history of floral needlework is so rich, every time period and every corner of the world is a virtual treasury of ideas. Sources range from the intricate designs of Oriental carpets to the simplified images of the early American samplers, from the complexity of the elegant rose to the stateliness of the lily. In short, the possibilities are astonishing, and the projects in this book are just a beginning.

♥

Each chapter features a main project—perhaps a sampler or a pillow—and an assortment of derivative projects using motifs from the main design. We know you'll be eager to pick other elements from the designs shown for creations of your own. To make it easier for you to come up with your own variations, for each project in the book, we've included information on using alternative fabrics with different counts.

♥

How does your garden grow? If you like to cross-stitch, you'll love the projects in this book, and you'll be able to cultivate an embroidered garden through the entire year.

Contents

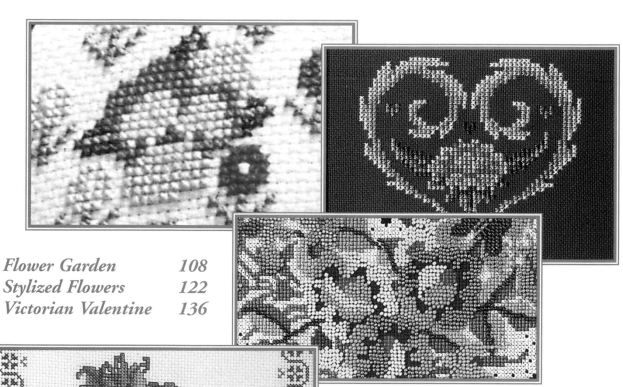

Spring Flowers

*F*ew events
are more exciting than seeing
the flowers of spring pop up
through the ground after a long
winter. As a signal of Earth's
reawakening, they gladden everyone's heart. Romance and
renewal are in the air, and each
new blossom provides a
breath of spring.

♥

Daffodils, pansies, primroses
and tulips are just a few of
the early blooms that inspired
our Spring Flowers Sampler. A
Daffodil Hatband trims a
fetching wide-brimmed straw
hat, and pansies cover a
Heart-shaped Box—perfect
for fragrant potpourri. A welcom-
ing floral Tea Tray invites
friends to celebrate spring with
a steaming cup of tea.

Spring Flowers Sampler
♥
Chart on pages 12-15

Materials
Stitched over two threads on 28-count Pistachio Pastel Linen (Zweigart #3234, #16). The fabric was cut 14" x 18". Finished size of framed sampler as shown is 12" x 16".

Stitch
Find and mark the center of the fabric. Line up the center of the chart with the center of the fabric. Follow the cross-stitch instructions given in Cross-Stitch Basics.

Finish
For best results, have this piece professionally matted and framed.

Alternate Design Sizes	
Stitches Per Inch	Design Sizes
11	14½" x 19"
14	11½" x 15"
18	9" x 11¾"
22	7½" x 9½"

Spring Flowers Sampler (upper left section)

SPRING FLOWERS KEY

Note: *Use 1 skein of all floss colors except DMC #905 and #3799, which require 2 skeins. Cross-stitch using 2 strands floss. Use 2 strands Marlitt and 2 strands floss where indicated.*

ANCHOR		DMC	COLOR
73		963	Ultra Vy. Lt. Dusty Rose
33	/	3708	Lt. Melon
28	□	893	Lt. Carnation
42	·	309	Deep Rose
1005	X	498	Dk. Christmas Red
129		3325	Lt. Baby Blue
203	(	964	Lt. Seagreen and 1052 Lt. Aqua Marlitt

ANCHOR		DMC	COLOR
187	O	958	Dk. Sea Green and 1053 Med. Aqua Marlitt
168	=	807	Peacock Blue
253		472	Ultra Lt. Avocado
255	+	907	Lt. Parrot Green
256	S	704	Brt. Chartreuse
264	\	3347	Med. Yellow Green
256	8	906	Med. Parrot Green
257	Y	905	Dk. Parrot Green
268	Z	3345	Dk. Hunter Green
1045		436	Tan
310	⊙	780	Ultra Vy. Dk. Topaz
359	●	801	Dk. Coffee Brown
2	·	WHITE	White

Spring Flowers Sampler (upper right section)

ANCHOR		DMC	COLOR
275		746	Off White
288	.•	445	Lt. Lemon
290	—	444	Dk. Lemon
279	‖	734	Lt. Olive Green
846	◇	3011	Dk. Khaki
900	⁒	648	Lt. Gray
96		554	Lt. Violet
98	~	553	Violet
99	✳	552	Med. Violet
941	◆	792	Dk. Cornflower
102	■	550	Vy. Dk. Violet
304	△	741	Med. Tangerine
204		913	Med. Nile Green
227	⌗	701	Lt. Christmas Green

ANCHOR		DMC	COLOR
		BACKSTITCH (Use 1 strand)	
236	⌐	3799	Vy. Dk. Pewter
		FRENCH KNOT (Use 2 strands/1 wrap)	
304	●	741	Med. Tangerine
236	●	3799	Vy. Dk. Pewter
		STRAIGHT STITCH (Use 1 strand)	
99	\	552	Med. Violet
		LAZY DAISY STITCH (Use 3 strands)	
290	⌀	444	Dk. Lemon

Overlap from adjacent section ↗

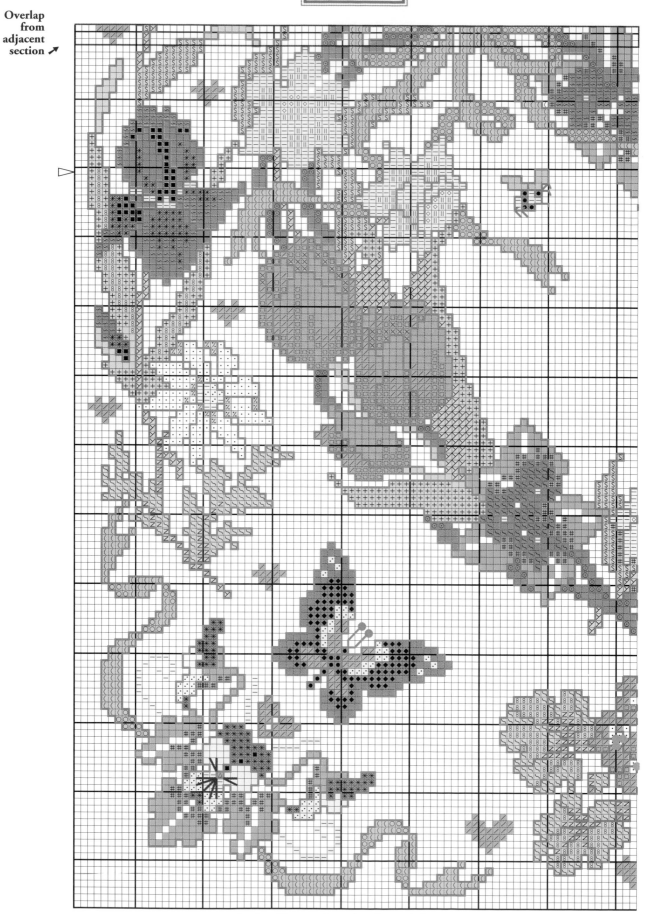

Spring Flowers Sampler (lower left section)

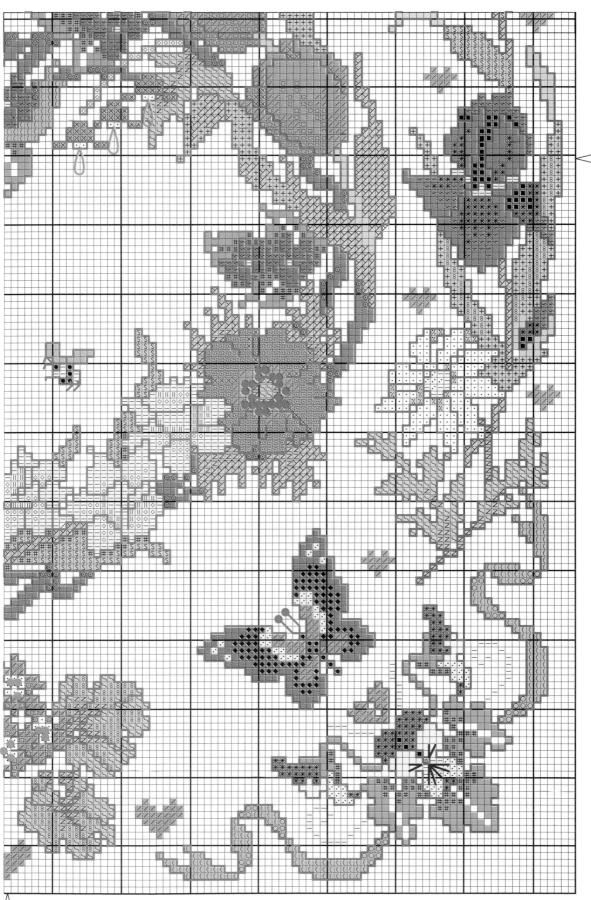

Overlap
from
adjacent
section

Spring Flowers Sampler (lower right section)

Tea Tray

♥

Charts on pages 17, 18

Materials

Stitched on 14-count White Aida (Zweigart #3706, #1). The fabric was cut 12" x 12". Finished size of tray insert is 10" x 10".

● Tray, 12½" x 12½" (Sudberry House #60138)

Stitch

Baste a marking line through the horizontal and vertical center of the fabric. Line up the quarter chart with the upper left quarter of the fabric. Work complete chart. Reverse the chart and complete the upper right quarter. Reverse the completed upper half to complete the lower half. Aligning shaded hearts with stitched hearts, work "Welcome" and "Friends" charts.

Finish

Following manufacturer's instructions, mount the cross-stitched piece in the tray.

Alternate Design Sizes	
Stitches Per Inch	Design Sizes
11	11½" x 11½"
14	9"x 9"
18	7" x 7"
22	5¾" x 5¾"

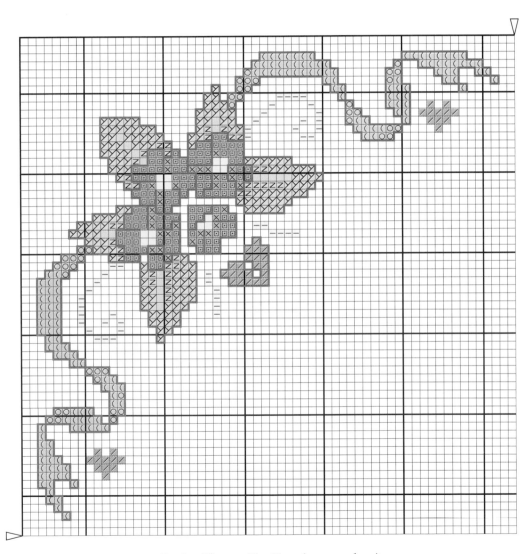

Spring Flowers Tea Tray (quarter chart)

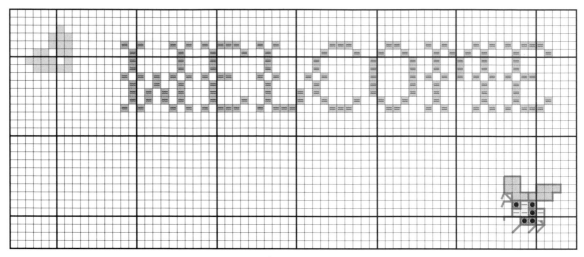

Spring Flowers Tea Tray

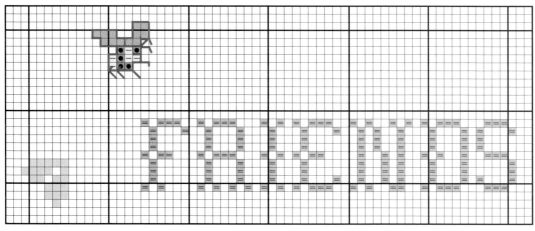

Spring Flowers Tea Tray

Daffodil Hatband

♥

Chart on page 21

Materials

Stitched on 14-count Aqua/White Cross-Stitch Band (Zweigart #7315, #161). The band was cut 2 yards long to allow for bow and streamers.

- White straw hat
- Small silk flower nosegay
- Craft glue
- Sewing thread to match fabric

Stitch

Find and mark the center of the band fabric. Line up the center row of the half chart with the center of the fabric. Working from the center out, work chart. Again working from the center, work the chart in reverse. Do not repeat the center row. Follow the cross-stitch instructions given in Cross-Stitch Basics.

Finish

Keeping the cross-stitched design centered, cut a 42-inch length of the band. Turn each end under twice; glue hems in place. With design at center front, wrap the band around

the hat, lapping and crisscrossing at center back and letting ends extend; glue in place. From remaining band cut two pieces, each 14 inches long, for bow loops. With right sides together, fold each length in half crosswise and sew the short ends together. Turn right side out. Flatten the loops, concealing the seam at center back. Glue the loops together, crisscrossing one over the other. Position the loops at center back of hat over the crisscrossed band; glue in place. Glue the nosegay over the loops.

Alternate Design Sizes	
Stitches Per Inch	Design Sizes
11	8" x 2"
14	6½" x 1½"
18	5" x 1¼"
22	4" x 1"

Heart-shaped Box
♥
Chart on page 21

Materials
Stitched over two threads on 28-count Pistachio Pastel Linen (Zweigart #3234, #16). The fabric was cut 7" x 7". Finished size of box lid is 5" x 5½".

● Fabric-covered heart box, 5" wide x 5½" long x 3" high
● White cotton rope-twist braid, ⅛" in diameter: 18"
● White sawtooth lace or eyelet edging, ⅜" wide: 18"
● Polyester batting
● Craft glue
● Fray Check™

Stitch
Find and mark the center of the fabric. Line up the center of the chart with the center of the fabric. Follow the cross-stitch instructions given in Cross-Stitch Basics.

Finish
Glue the lace around the edge of the top of the heart box, having the sawtooth edges extend beyond the box. Turn under and lap the raw edges. Cut the batting to the same dimensions as the top of the heart box. Cut the cross-stitched fabric ¼ inch larger all around. Turn the edges under ¼ inch, over the batting, and glue to secure; press. Glue to the top of the box. Glue the braid over inner edge of the lace. Dab ends of braid with Fray Check™ to prevent fraying.

Alternate Design Sizes	
Stitches Per Inch	Design Sizes
11	4½" x 4"
14	3½" x 3¼"
18	2¾" x 2½"
22	2¼" x 2"

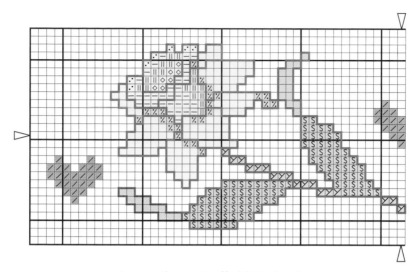

Spring Flowers Daffodil Hatband

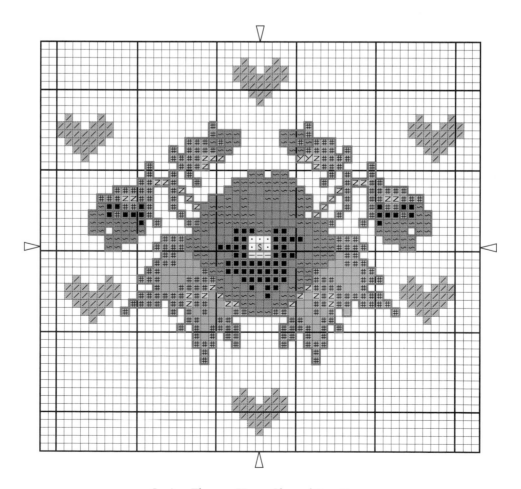

Spring Flowers Heart-Shaped Box Top

A Child's Garden

"Mary, Mary, quite contrary, how does your garden grow? With silver bells and cockle shells and pretty maids all in a row."

♥

Whether it's the setting for a little girl's first tea party or the scene of a playful game of ring-around-the-rosy, gardens can be enchanted places for children. The beauty and bounty of nature provide a magical place to play and dream in.

♥

The Childhood Flowers Sampler has all the ingredients needed to awaken the child in anyone—a charming cottage surrounded by favorite flowers and friendly bunnies and birds. Motifs taken from the main design are used to create a Birth-Date Pillow, a Doll's Pinafore, and a dainty Tablecloth and Napkin just right for a summer tea-party table.

A Child's Garden Sampler

Chart on pages 26-29

Materials

Stitched over two threads on 28-count Cream Pastel Linen (Zweigart #3234, #12). The fabric was cut 14" x 19". Finished size of framed sampler as shown is 12½"x 17¼".

Stitch

Find and mark the center of the fabric. Line up the center of the chart with the center of the fabric. Follow the cross-stitch instructions given in Cross-Stitch Basics.

Finish

For best results, have this piece professionally matted and framed.

Alternate Design Sizes	
Stitches Per Inch	Design Sizes
11	12½" x 17½"
14	9¾" x 13¾"
18	7½" x 10½"
22	6" x 8 ¾"

A Child's Garden Sampler (upper left section)

A CHILD'S GARDEN KEY

Note: *Use 1 skein of all floss colors except DMC #899, #727, #704, #905, and #742, which require 2. Cross-stitch using 2 strands floss.*

ANCHOR		DMC	COLOR
24	/	776	Med. Pink
52	◯	899	Med. Rose
59	+	3350	Ultra Dk. Dusty Rose
89	✕	917	Med. Plum
1028	●	3685	Dk. Mauve
264	·	3348	Lt. Yellow Green
256	/	704	Bright Chartreuse
214	◯	368	Lt. Pistachio
257	☐	905	Dk. Parrot Green
226	✕	702	Kelly Green
268	●	3345	Dk. Hunter Green
246	■	986	Vy. Dk. Forest Green

ANCHOR		DMC	COLOR
342	/	211	Lt. Lavender
110	◯	208	Vy. Dk. Lavender
109	+	209	Dk. Lavender
102	■	550	Vy. Dk. Violet
158	·	747	Vy. Lt. Sky Blue
167	/	598	Lt. Turquoise
129	◯	3325	Lt. Baby Blue
977	✕	334	Med. Baby Blue
162	●	825	Dk. Blue
275	·	746	Off White
293	/	727	Vy. Lt. Topaz
302	◯	743	Med. Yellow
874	☐	834	Vy. Lt. Golden Olive
304	✕	741	Med. Tangerine
277	●	831	Med. Golden Olive
399	◯	318	Lt. Steel Gray
400	✕	317	Pewter Gray

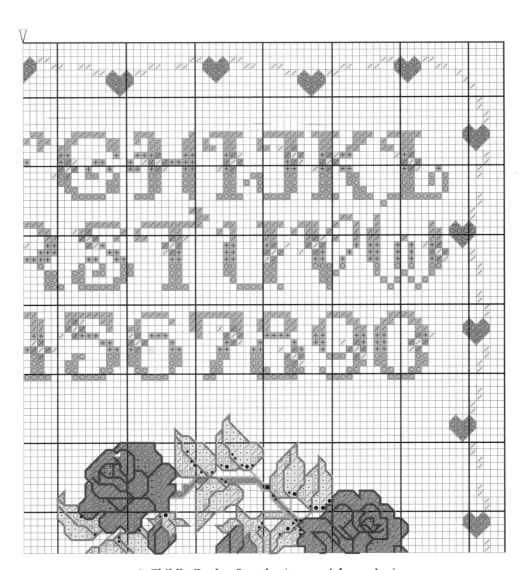

A Child's Garden Sampler (upper right section)

ANCHOR		DMC	COLOR
403	■	310	Black
2	•	WHITE	White
830	·	644	Med. Beige Gray
1045	□	436	Tan
903	✕	640	Vy. Dk. Beige Gray
944	●	869	Vy. Dk. Hazel Nut
887	╱	3046	Med. Yellow Beige
1049	○	301	Med. Mahogany
352	+	300	Vy. Dk. Mahogany
359	■	801	Dk. Coffee Brown
		FRENCH KNOT (strands/wrap)	
59	●	3350	Ultra Dk. Dusty Rose (2/1)
382	●	3371	Black Brown (2/1)
2	○	WHITE	White (1/1)
256	●	704	Bright Chartreuse (2/1)

ANCHOR		DMC	COLOR
293	○	727	Vy. Lt. Topaz (2/1)
293	○	727	Vy. Lt. Topaz (2/2)
52	●	899	Med. Rose (2/1)
		STRAIGHT STITCH	
303	╱	742	Lt. Tangerine, 2 strands
256	╱	704	Bright Chartreuse, 1 strand
102	╲	550	Vy. Dk. Violet, 1 strand
		BACKSTITCH (Use 1 strand)	
382	┗	3371	Black Brown
862	┗	934	Black Avocado Green
906	┗	829	Vy. Dk. Golden Olive
352	┗	300	Vy. Dk. Mahogany
400	┗	317	Pewter Gray
102	┗	550	Vy. Dk. Violet

**Overlap
from
adjacent
section** ↗

A Child's Garden Sampler (lower left section)

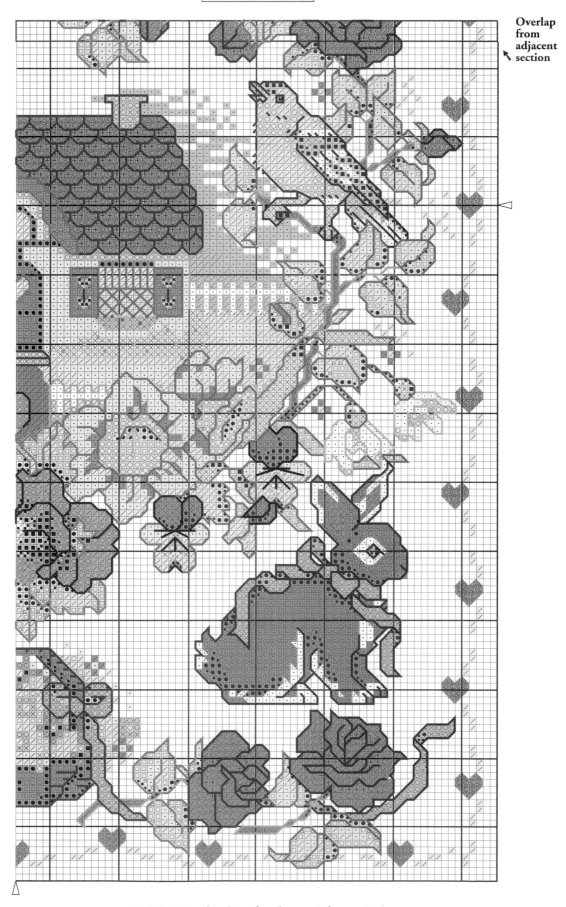

Overlap
from
adjacent
section

A Child's Garden Sampler (lower right section)

Tablecloth

♥

Chart on page 31

Materials

Stitched over two threads on 28-count Cream Pastel Linen (Zweigart #3234, #12). The fabric was cut 24" x 24". Finished size of tablecloth is 23" x 23", plus edging.

● Cream Cluny-type lace edging, ⅝" wide: 2¾ yards
● Thread to match fabric

Stitch

At each corner of the fabric, measure and mark a point 1½ inches from each edge. Begin counting from the outlined outer corner of the border chart at this point. Work the cross-stitch design in each corner of the tablecloth. Follow the cross-stitch instructions given in Cross-Stitch Basics.

Finish

Turn each edge of the tablecloth ½ inch to the wrong side; press. With right sides facing up, lap the pressed edges just over the lace edging all around, allowing the lace to peek out as much as possible. Pin lace in place, folding corners neatly to miter, and lapping ends. Stitch in place.

Alternate Design Sizes

Stitches Per Inch	Design Sizes
11	6¾" x 6¾"
14	5¼" x 5¼"
18	4" x 4"
22	3½" x 3½"

A Child's Garden Tablecloth (corner chart)

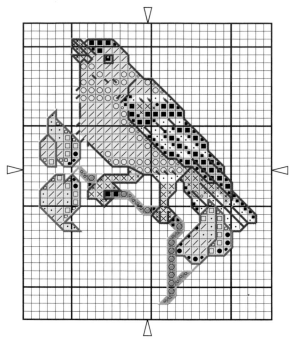

A Child's Garden Napkin

Napkin
♥
Chart shown above

Materials
(For one napkin)
Stitched over two threads on 28-count Cream Pastel Linen (Zweigart #3234, #12). The fabric was cut 12" x 12". Finished size of napkin is 11" x 11", plus edging.

● Cream Cluny-type lace, ⅝" wide: 48"

Stitch
In the lower left corner of the fabric, baste the outline of an area 2 inches x 2½ inches, approximately 1 inch in from edges. Find and mark the center of the thread-marked

area. Line up the center of the Napkin chart with the center of the marked area. Follow the cross-stitch instructions given in Cross-Stitch Basics.

Finish
Finish as for tablecloth, above.

Alternate Design Sizes	
Stitches Per Inch	Design Sizes
11	2¾" x 3½"
14	2" x 2¾"
18	1 ¾ " x 2"
22	1½" x 1¾"

Birth-Date Pillow

♥

Chart on pages 26-29

Materials

Stitched over two threads on 28-count Cream Pastel Linen (Zweigart #3234, #12). The fabric was cut 14½" x 29". Finished size of pillow is 13½" x 13½".

- Fusible interfacing: 14½" x 14½"
- Pink loop braid: 1¾ yards
- Polyester stuffing
- Sewing thread to match fabric

Stitch

Cut the linen in half to make two 14½-inch squares. Find and mark the center of one square for the pillow top. Using the center heart wreath motif from the sampler chart, omit the house and lawn and substitute the child's name and date of birth. See alphabet, page 35. Line up the center of the motif with the center of one piece of the fabric. Work the cross-stitch design on the pillow top, following the cross-stitch instructions given in Cross-Stitch Basics.

Finish

Following manufacturer's instructions, fuse the interfacing to the wrong side of the cross-stitched pillow top. Pin, then baste, the loop braid around the edge of the right side of the pillow top all around, having the loops face toward the center and matching edges; lap ends of braid. With right sides together, pin the pillow top to the back. Stitch around 3 sides and 4 corners, taking a ½-inch seam and leaving an opening for turning. Grade seam allowances and trim corners, turn right side out, and stuff. Slipstitch the opening closed.

Alternate Design Sizes	
Stitches Per Inch	Design Sizes
11	11¾" x 9¾"
14	9¼" x 7½"
18	7¼" x 6"
22	6" x 5"

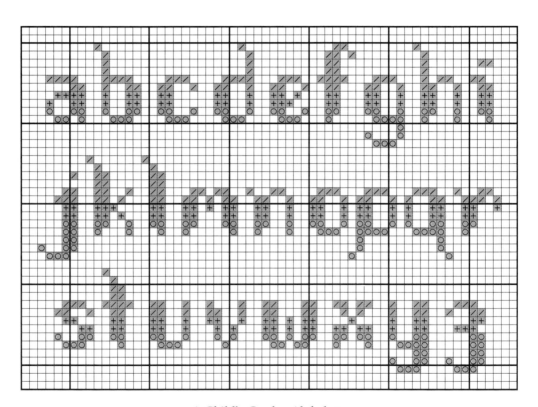

A Child's Garden Alphabet

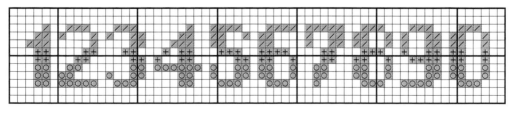

A Child's Garden Numbers

Doll's Pinafore

♥

Materials

Stitched on 14-count White Damask Aida (Zweigart #3229, #1). The pinafore shown here requires ½ yard of fabric, and measures 14" around waist and 11" in length from shoulder to hem.

- White flat lace edging, ⅝" wide: approximately 1½ yards
- Lining fabric

- White satin ribbon, ⅜" wide: 1½ yards
- Dressmaker's pencil
- Sewing thread to match fabric

Cut

NOTE: All measurements include ½-inch seam allowances.

Measure the doll's waist. Add 11 inches to this measurement for the skirt width. Determine desired skirt length and add 1 inch. Then cut a rectangle of Damask Aida to these measurements for the pinafore skirt (see Figure 1). Cut a piece of lining fabric the same size. For pinafore bib, measure the doll's chest height from waist to shoulder (see Figure 2) and add 1 inch; then measure across front of chest from shoulder to shoulder (see Figure 2) and add 1 inch. Cut Damask Aida to these measurements. To shape neckline, fold bib in half lengthwise and mark a curve as shown in Figure 3; cut out. Using this piece as a pattern, cut bib lining. Remaining pieces will be cut later.

Stitch

Find and mark the center of the Damask Aida pinafore bib. Using the basket motif from the sampler chart, line up the center of the motif with the center of the fabric. Work the cross-stitch design, following the cross-stitch instructions given in Cross-Stitch Basics.

Finish

NOTE: Unless specified otherwise, stitch pieces with right sides together, taking ½-inch seams. Turn lower edge of skirt under ½ inch; press. Lap this edge over a length of lace edging cut to fit; stitch in place. Press and stitch narrow hems along each side edge of skirt. Mark center of top edge. Gather top edge of skirt to fit doll's waist. Adjust gathers evenly and secure gathering threads.

Measure doll's back from shoulder to back waist and add 1 inch. Cut two strips to this length x 1¾ inches wide, for shoulder straps. Fold each strip in half lengthwise and stitch along long edges and across one end. Trim seam allowances, turn right side out, and press. Cut two pieces of lace edging to fit side edges of cross-stitched bib. Finish one short end of each (the upper end) with a narrow hem or zigzag stitching. With right side of bib facing up, matching raw ends to shoulder edges of bib, center and pin shoulder straps to shoulder edges of bib. Then, matching edges and placing finished ends at shoulders, pin a length of lace along each side edge of bib (see Figure 4). Baste lace and straps in place. Pin lining over bib, with lace and straps in between; ends of straps should extend from bottom edge of bib. Leaving bottom edge of bib open, stitch side, shoulder, and neckline edges. Grade seam allowances, clip curves and trim corners. Turn bib right side out; press. Mark center of lower edge. Matching center markings, pin lower edge of bib to gathered edge of skirt; stitch in place. Press seam allowances and bib toward shoulders.

continued

For waistband, cut a strip of Aida cloth 1¾ inches wide and long enough to fit gathered edge of skirt, plus 1 inch; cut waistband lining the same. Press and stitch a narrow hem along each short end of waistband. Press one long edge under ½ inch. Pin unpressed long edge of waistband to gathered edge of skirt; stitch in place (see Figure 5). Press waistband up over bib; stitch in place. Hem ends of waistband lining as for waistband, and press both long edges under ½ inch. On wrong side of pinafore, pin lining to waistband and skirt (see Figure 6). Leaving ends open, slipstitch upper and lower edges of lining in place, forming a tube. Draw ribbon through tube to use as ties. Try pinafore on doll: Pin ends of shoulder straps to inside of waistband at back and adjust to fit; tack straps in place, or, if preferred, sew on snap fasteners.

Alternate Design Sizes	
Stitches Per Inch	Design Sizes
11	3½" x 2¼"
14	2¾" x 1¾"
18	2¼" x 1½"
22	1¾" x 1¼"

Doll Pinafore Patterns

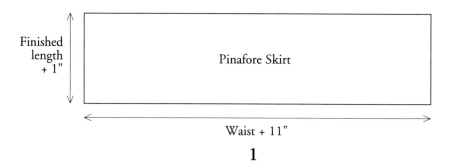

Finished length + 1"

Pinafore Skirt

Waist + 11"

1

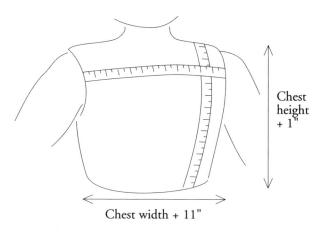

Chest height + 1"

Chest width + 11"

2

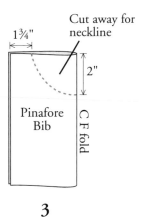

Cut away for
neckline

1¾"

2"

Pinafore
Bib

C F fold

3

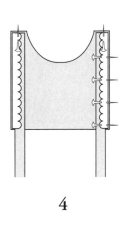

4

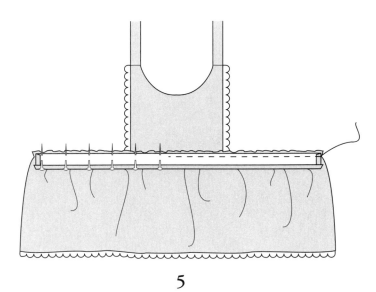

5

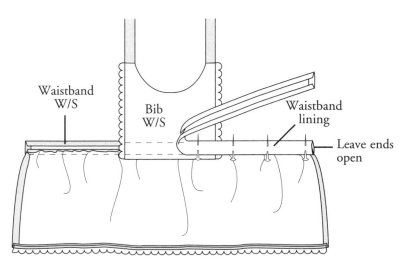

Waistband
W/S

Bib
W/S

Waistband
lining

Leave ends
open

6

Wildflower Garden

Wildflowers are nature's paint palette. From early spring to the first hard frost, wildflowers add an ever-changing variety of color and texture to the landscape. Beginning with the first tiny violets of spring and continuing through summer to bright fields of autumn asters, nature provides us with a landscape rich in visual gifts.

♥

Favorite wildflowers include iris, morning glories, black-eyed Susans, and poppies. Stitch this lush bedroom set and have a wildflower garden in your home all year 'round. A border of ivy surrounds the flower-filled heart at the center of the Wildflower Garden Pillow. The Bolster Pillow, Pillowcase Borders, Hand Mirror and Trinket Box Lid use floral elements from the main design, while the Sachet repeats the ivy motif.

Wildflower Pillow

♥

Chart on pages 45-53

Materials

Stitched over two threads on 28-count Ice Blue Annabelle (Zweigart #3240, #550). The fabric was cut 18" x 18". Finished size of pillow is 16" x 16".

- White fabric for pillow back: ½ yard
- Pregathered white eyelet edging, 3" wide: 2 yards
- Fusible interfacing: 17" x 17"
- Pillow form: 16" square (or use polyester stuffing)
- Sewing thread to match fabric

Stitch

Find and mark the center of the fabric. Line up the center of the chart with the center of the fabric. Follow the cross-stitch instructions given in Cross-Stitch Basics.

Finish

Trim cross-stitched pillow top to 17 inches square. Following manufacturer's instructions, fuse the interfacing to the wrong side of the cross-stitched pillow top. Cut pillow back fabric same size as top; set aside.

Join ends of eyelet edging with a French seam to form a ring. With seam at center of one side, and with right sides together, pin eyelet around edges of pillow top, with ruffle facing center of pillow top. Machine-baste all around.

With right sides together, pin the pillow top to the back, enclosing the ruffle. Taking a ½ inch seam, stitch around 3 sides and 4 corners, leaving an opening for turning. Grade seam allowances, trim corners, and turn right side out. Insert the pillow form or stuff with polyester stuffing. Slipstitch the opening closed.

Alternate Design Sizes	
Stitches Per Inch	Design Sizes
11	20½" x 19½"
14	16" x 15½"
18	12½" x 12"
22	10¼" x 9¾"

WILDFLOWER GARDEN KEY

Note: *Use 1 skein of all floss colors except DMC #989, #988, and #986, which require 2 each. Cross-stitch using 2 strands floss for all projects except Trinket Box. Trinket Box requires 1 strand floss.*

ANCHOR	DMC	COLOR
342	211	Lt. Lavender
108	210	Med. Lavender
96	554	Lt. Violet
110	208	Vy. Dk. Lavender
98	553	Violet
99	552	Med. Violet
102	550	Very Dk. Violet
23	818	Baby Pink
73	963	Ultra Vy. Lt. Dusty Rose
75	962	Med. Dusty Rose
144	801	Dk. Coffee Brown
380	838	Vy. Dk. Beige Brown
307	783	Med. Topaz
308	782	Dk. Topaz
304	741	Med. Tangerine
316	971	Pumpkin
334	606	Brt. Orange Red
332	608	Bright Orange
215	320	Med. Pistachio
217	367	Dk. Pistachio
218	319	Vy. Dk. Pistachio
300	745	Lt. Pale Yellow
305	725	Topaz
302	743	Med. Yellow
298	972	Deep Canary
118	340	Blue Violet
1030	3746	Dk. Blue Violet
242	989	Forest Green
243	988	Med. Forest Green
246	986	Vy. Dk. Forest Green
253	472	Ultra Lt. Avocado Green
264	3348	Lt. Yellow Green
267	470	Lt. Avocado Green
266	471	Vy. Lt. Avocado Green
267	469	Avocado Green
860	522	Fern Green
862	520	Dk. Fern Green
858	524	Vy. Lt. Fern Green

ANCHOR	DMC	COLOR
842	3013	Lt. Khaki Green
844	3012	Med. Khaki Green
846	3011	Dk. Khaki Green
117	341	Lt. Blue Violet
977	334	Med. Baby Blue
926	712	Cream
403	310	Black

BACKSTITCH (Use 1 strand)

ANCHOR	DMC	COLOR	
1005	816	Garnet	Poppy
42	309	Deep Rose	Wild Roses
1015	3777	Vy. Dk. Terra Cotta	Black-Eyed Susan, Mexican Sunflower
862	934	Black Avocado Green	Tendrils, Leaf Veins, Buttercup Buds, Heart
941	792	Dk. Cornflower Blue	Starflowers, Morning Glory
118	340	Med. Blue Violet	Outer Border
302	743	Med. Yellow	Outer Border
310	780	Ultra Vy. Dk. Topaz	Yellow Primrose, Buttercups
403	310	Black	Poppy Center
119	333	Vy. Dk. Blue Violet	Wood Violet
102	550	Vy. Dk. Violet	Iris

FRENCH KNOTS (2 strands/1 wrap)

ANCHOR	DMC	COLOR	
305	725	Topaz	Morning Glory

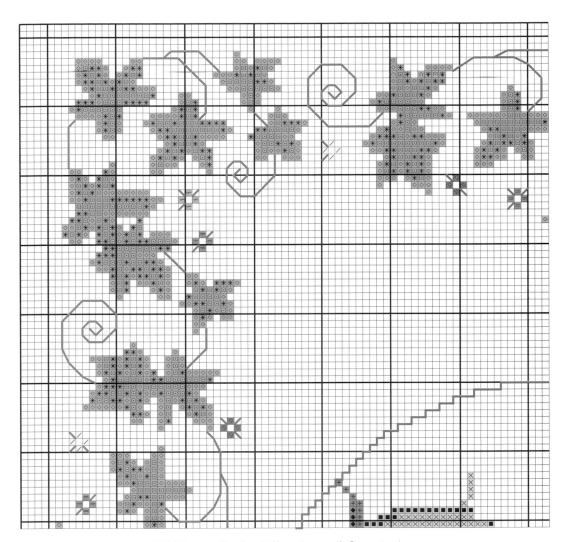

Wildflower Garden Pillow (upper left section)

upper left	upper center	upper right
center left	center	center right
lower left	lower center	lower right

**Overlap
from
adjacent
section →**

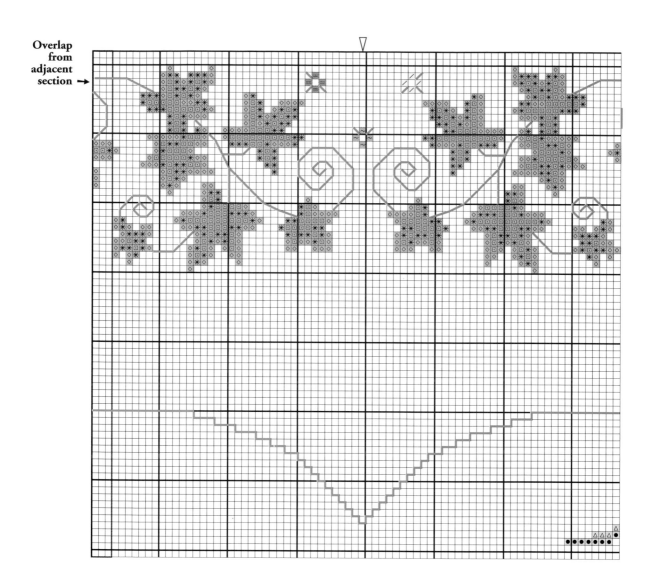

Wildflower Garden Pillow (upper center section)

upper left	upper center	upper right
center right	center	center right
lower left	lower center	lower right

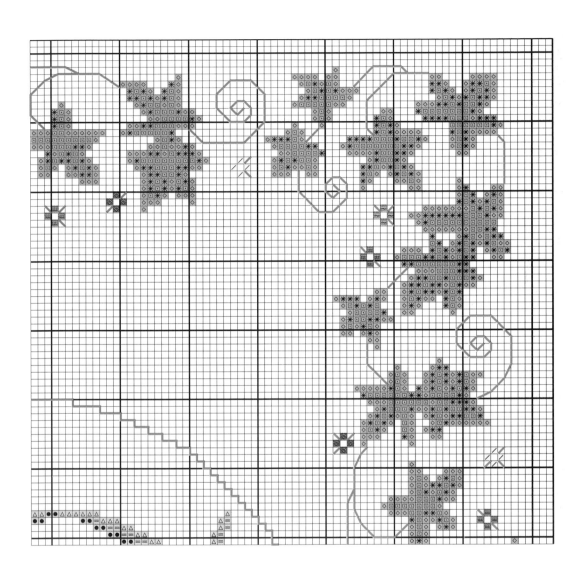

Wildflower Garden Pillow (upper right section)

Overlap from adjacent section ↗

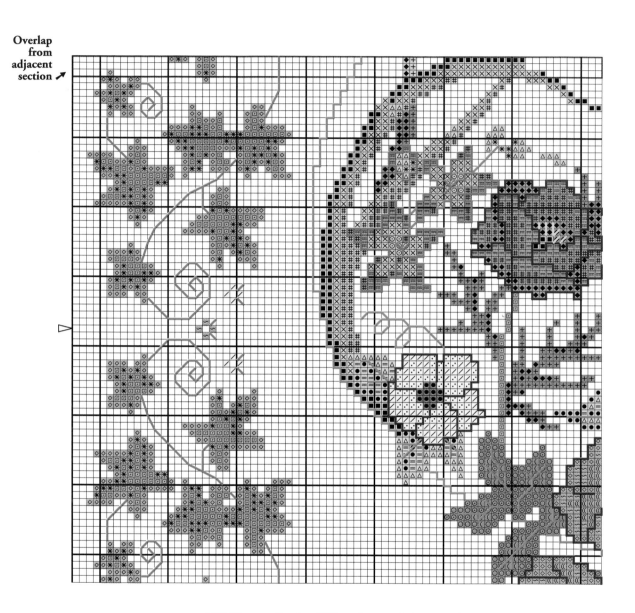

Wildflower Garden Pillow (center left section)

upper left	upper center	upper right
center left	center	center right
lower left	lower center	lower right

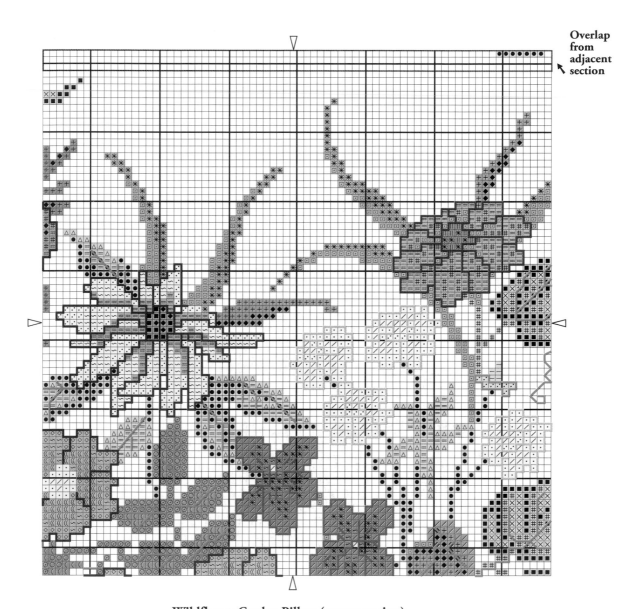

**Overlap
from
adjacent
section**

Wildflower Garden Pillow (center section)

**Overlap
from
adjacent
section**

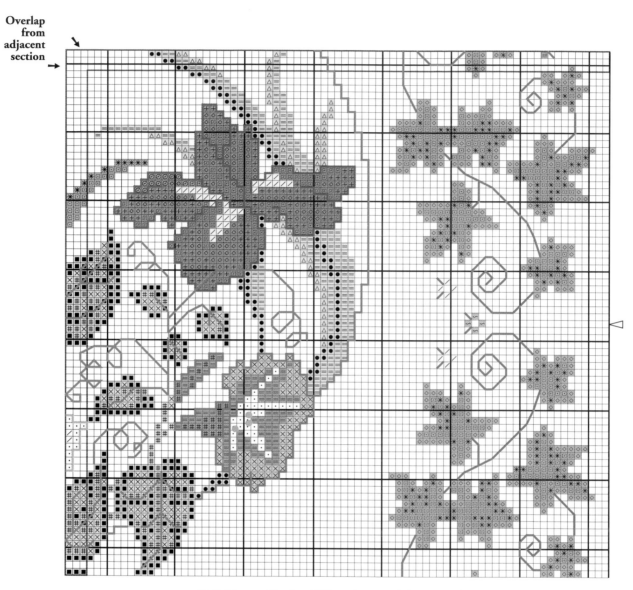

Wildflower Garden Pillow (center right section)

upper left	upper center	upper right
center right	center	center right
lower left	lower center	lower right

Wildflower Garden Pillow (lower right section)

Overlap from adjacent section ←

**Overlap
from
adjacent
section** ↗

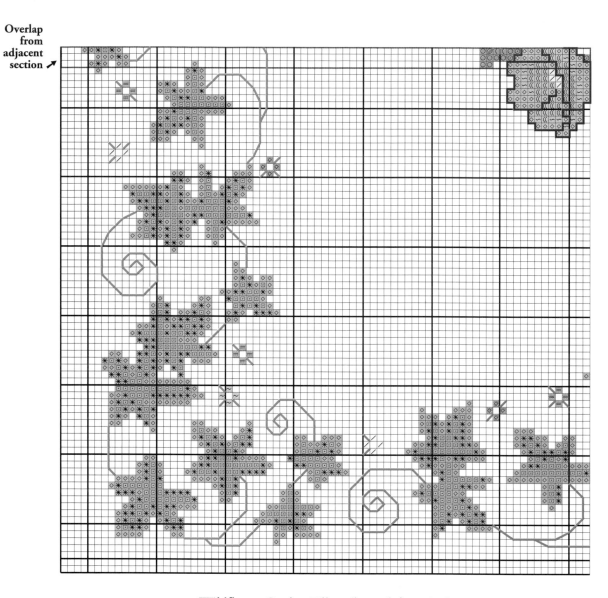

Wildflower Garden Pillow (lower left section)

upper left	upper center	upper right
center right	center	center right
lower left	lower center	lower right

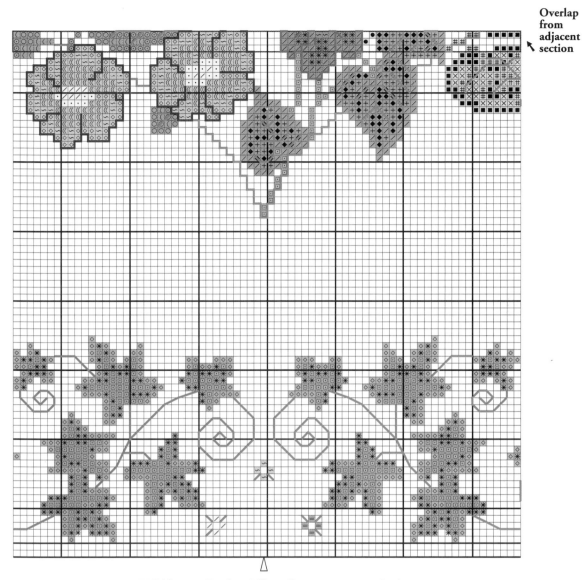

Overlap from adjacent section

Wildflower Garden Pillow (lower center section)

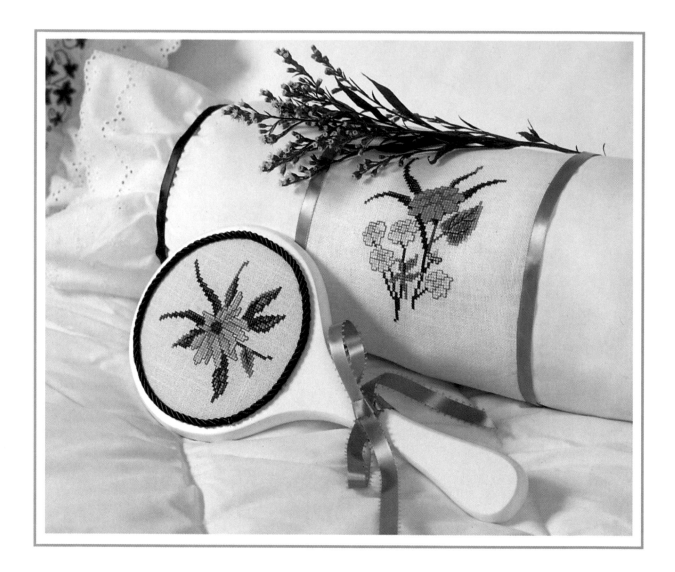

Hand Mirror

♥

Chart on page 55

Materials

Stitched over two threads on 28-count Ice Blue Annabelle (Zweigart #3240, #550). The fabric was cut 7" x 7". Finished size of hand mirror is 5½" in diameter.

● Hand mirror: 6" x 12" (Sudberry House #23302)
● Batting: 6" x 6"

- Dark Green twisted satin braid, ¼" in diameter: 19"
- Fray Check™
- Craft glue

Stitch

Find and mark the center of the fabric. Line up the center of the Hand Mirror chart with the center of the fabric. Follow the cross-stitch instructions given in Cross-Stitch Basics.

Finish

Keeping the design centered, trim the fabric and the batting to a circle 6 inches in diameter. Following the mirror manufacturer's instructions, mount the fabric over the batting in the hand mirror. Cut the braid to fit around the edge of the cross-stitched piece and glue in place. Dab ends of the braid with Fray Check™ to prevent fraying.

Alternate Design Sizes	
Stitches Per Inch	Design Sizes
11	3½" x 4½"
14	2¾" x 3½"
18	2" x 2¾"
22	1¾" x 2¼"

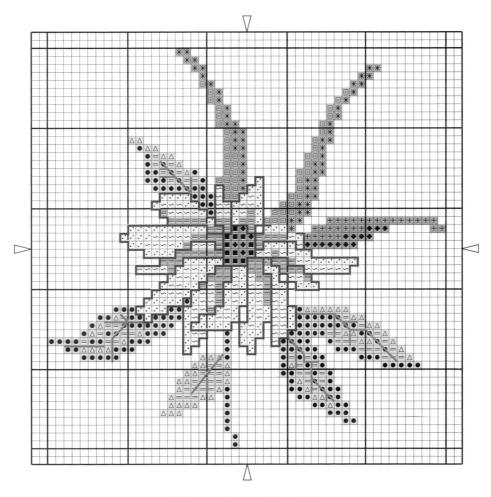

Wildflower Garden Hand Mirror

Bolster Pillow

♥

Chart on page 57

Materials

Stitched over two threads on 28-count White Cashel Linen 28 (Zweigart #3281, #100). The fabric was cut 7" x 20". Finished bolster size is 6" in diameter x 16" long, plus eyelet trim.

- White fabric to complete bolster, 45" wide: ½ yard
- Flat white eyelet trim, 5" wide: 54"
- Double-faced satin ribbon, ⅜" wide: 1¼ yards each Sage and Dark Green
- Neck bolster pillow form, 6" in diameter x 16" long
- Dressmaker's pencil
- Sewing thread to match fabric

Stitch

Find and mark the center of the fabric. The long edges of the fabric will be at the sides of the design. Line up the center of the Bolster Pillow chart with the center of the fabric. Follow the cross-stitch instructions given in Cross-Stitch Basics.

Finish

NOTE: Join pieces with right sides together, taking ½-inch seams; press seam allowances open.

From the white fabric, cut 2 rectangles, each 6 x 20 inches. Then draw 2 circles, each 7 inches in diameter, on the remaining fabric and cut out for bolster ends. Stitch one rectangle to each long edge of the cross-stitched center piece. Fold in half, perpen-dicular to the seams, and stitch together for 1 inch at each end, to form the bolster tube. Leave the center section open for inserting the pillow form (see Figure 1). Turn the bolster tube right side out.

Cut the eyelet in half to make 2 pieces, each 27 inches long. Stitch 2 rows of gathering stitches along the selvage or unfinished edge of each piece, leaving long thread ends. Join ends of each piece with a French seam to form a ring. Pull threads to gather so the eyelet ruffle measures about 19 inches. Do not turn right side out. Pin an eyelet ruffle to each end of the bolster tube with the ruffle facing toward the center, adjusting gathers as necessary. Machine-baste in place (see Figure 2). Turn tube wrong side out, tucking ruffle inside. Slip a circular bolster end into one end of the bolster tube, sandwiching the ruffle in the middle. Pin, then stitch all around (see Figure 3). Repeat at other end. Turn right side out. Insert pillow form and slipstitch the opening closed. Cut 2 lengths of sage ribbon each 20 inches long. Fold each in half, sew the ends together, and turn right side out. Position one ribbon ring over each edge of the cross-stitched center section, directly over the seam, and sew in place. In the same manner, prepare and sew the dark green ribbon around each end seam of the bolster.

Alternate Design Sizes	
Stitches Per Inch	Design Sizes
11	4½" x 6"
14	3½" x 4¾"
18	2¾" x 3¾"
22	2¼" x 3"

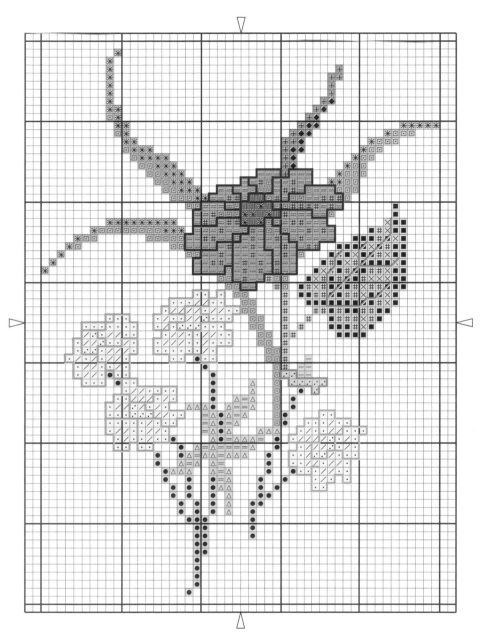

Wildflower Garden Bolster Pillow

Bolster Pillow

Leave open

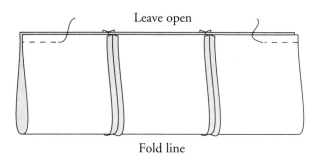

Fold line

1

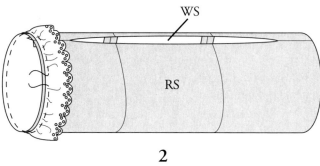

WS

RS

2

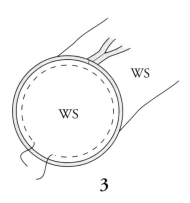

WS

WS

WS

3

Trinket Box

♥

Chart on page 60

Materials

Stitched over two threads on 18-count Forget-Me-Not Blue Aida (Wichelt #358-103). The fabric was cut 5" x 5". Finished size of trinket box lid is 3½" in diameter.

● Trinket Box (Anne Brinkley Designs)

Stitch

Find and mark the center of the fabric. Line up the center of the Trinket Box chart with the center of the fabric. Follow the cross-stitch instructions given in Cross-Stitch Basics.

continued

Finish

Keeping the design centered, trim the embroidered fabric to a circle 3½ inches in diameter. Following manufacturer's instructions, mount the fabric to the top of the trinket box.

Alternate Design Sizes	
Stitches Per Inch	Design Sizes
9	4" x 4 ¼"
11	3¼" x 3½"
14	2½" x 2¾"
18	2" x 2"
22	1½" x 1¾"

Sachet

♥

Chart on page 61

Materials

Stitched over two threads on 28-count Ice Blue Annabelle (Zweigart #3240, #550). The fabric was cut 11" x 4". Finished size of sachet is 5" x 7", including lace.

- Flat white eyelet trim, 4" wide: 11"
- Bright blue satin ribbon, ⅜" wide: 30"
- Potpourri
- Sewing thread to match fabric

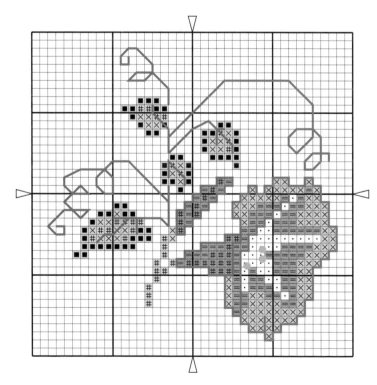

Wildflower Garden Trinket Box

Stitch

Find and mark the center of the fabric. The long edges of the fabric will be at the top and bottom of the design. Line up the center of the ivy chart with the center of the marked fabric. Follow the cross-stitch instructions given in Cross-Stitch Basics.

Finish

NOTE: Stitch ½-inch seams and press seam allowances open.

With right sides together, stitch the eyelet trim to the upper long edge of the cross-stitched piece. Fold the piece in half crosswise with the right side facing in and stitch the short edges together to form a tube. Position this seam at center back of the sachet. With the right side facing in, stitch the remaining raw edges of the cross-stitched piece together for the bottom of the sachet. Turn right side out. Fill with potpourri as desired and tie the top closed with the ribbon. Trim ends of ribbon at an angle.

Alternate Design Sizes	
Stitches Per Inch	Design Sizes
11	2¾" x 6"
14	2" x 4½"
18	1¾" x 3½"
22	1½" x 3"

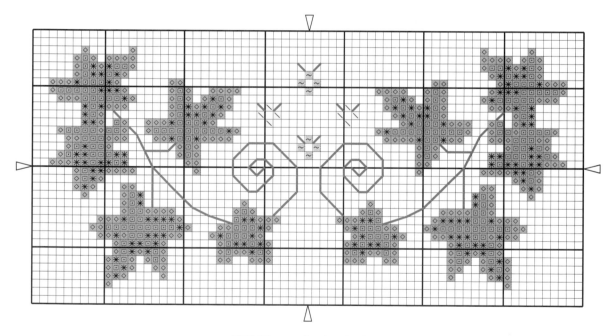

Wildflower Garden Sachet

Pillowcase

♥

Chart on page 63

Materials

Stitched over two threads on 28-count White Cashel Linen (Zweigart #3281, #100). The fabric was cut 21" x 7". Finished pillowcase size is 20" x 31".

- White fabric for pillowcase: 1½ yards
- Flat white eyelet trim, 2½" wide: 42"
- Double-faced satin ribbon, ⅜" wide: 21" each Sage and Dark Green
- Sewing thread to match fabric

Stitch

Find and mark the center of the fabric. The long edges of the fabric will be at the sides of the design. Line up the center of the Pillowcase chart with the center of the fabric. Follow the cross-stitch instructions given in Cross-Stitch Basics.

Finish

NOTE: Join pieces with right sides together, taking ½-inch seams; press seam allowances open.

Cut a rectangle of white fabric 51 inches long x 21 inches wide. Stitch one long edge of the cross-stitched piece to one short edge of the white fabric. Cut the eyelet in half, and stitch one piece to the other long edge of the cross-stitched piece and the second eyelet piece to the other short edge of the white fabric. On the front of the pillowcase, position and sew the sage ribbon directly over the seam that joins the cross-stitched fabric to the backing; sew the dark green ribbon over the seam that joins the cross-stitched fabric to the eyelet, as pictured. Now fold the pieced pillowcase in half crosswise, wrong side out, bringing the edges with the eyelet together. Leaving the eyelet-edged end open, stitch the long side edges together. Turn right side out.

Alternate Design Sizes	
Stitches Per Inch	Design Sizes
11	2¾" x 4"
14	2¼" x 3"
18	1¾" x 2½"
22	1½" x 2"

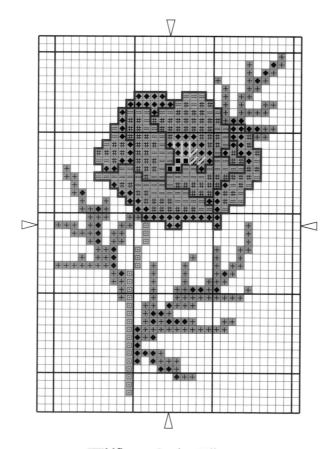

Wildflower Garden Pillowcase

Wedding Flowers

*S*urely no occasion links romance and flowers more completely than a wedding. Create a treasured hearts-and-flowers memento for that most special day in your life, or for someone dear to you who will be walking down the aisle.

♥

Flowers and ribbons in delicate colors are intertwined to form a fabulous heart-shaped bridal wreath, and opalescent threads add sparkle to this beautiful Wedding Sampler, stitched on crisp white Quaker Cloth. Blossoms from the wreath adorn the Ring Bearer's Pillow and Bride's Handkerchief. The Floral Border Frame makes a perfect wedding gift, while the dainty Heart Charm serves as a pretty table favor.

Wedding Sampler

♥

Chart on pages 68-72

Materials

Stitched over two threads on 28-count White Quaker Cloth (Zweigart #3993, #100). The fabric was cut 13" x 18". Finished sampler size is 11" x 16".

Stitch

Find and mark the center of the fabric. Line up the center of the chart with the center of the fabric. Use two strands of floss to work the cross-stitch design. Use two strands of floss to backstitch the words and border and one strand to backstitch the wreath. Where indicated on the Key, work one strand of Kreinik Blending Filament together with two strands of floss. Follow the cross-stitch instructions given in Cross-Stitch Basics.

Work names and date following instructions given in Cross-Stitch Basics.

Finish

For best results, have this piece professionally matted and framed.

Alternate Design Sizes	
Stitches Per Inch	Design Sizes
11	13" x 18¾"
14	10¼" x 14¾"
18	8" x 11½"
22	6½" x 9½"

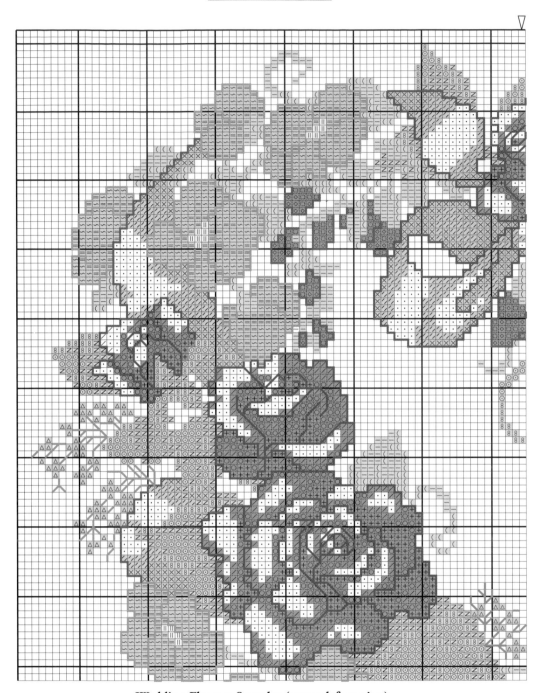

Wedding Flowers Sampler (upper left section)

WEDDING FLOWERS KEY

Note: *Use 1 skein of all floss colors. Cross-stitch using 2 strands floss. Use 1 strand Kreinik Blending Filament with 2 strands floss where indicated.*

ANCHOR		DMC	COLOR
271	◇	819	Lt. Baby Pink
1026	╱	225	Vy. Lt. Shell Pink
49	○	3689	Lt. Mauve
6	□	353	Peach Flesh
66	+	3688	Med. Mauve
1037	⌣	3756	Vy. Lt. Baby Blue
160	=	827	Vy. Lt. Blue

ANCHOR		DMC	COLOR
144	⁄⁄	800	Pale Delft and Kreinik 095 Starburst
117	△	341	Lt. Blue Violet and Kreinik 093 Star Mauve
130	✕	809	Delft and Kreinik 095 Starburst
1043	⊙	369	Vy. Lt. Pistachio
206	—	966	Med. Baby Green
876	8	503	Med. Blue Green
215	(	320	Med. Pistachio
877	Z	502	Blue-green

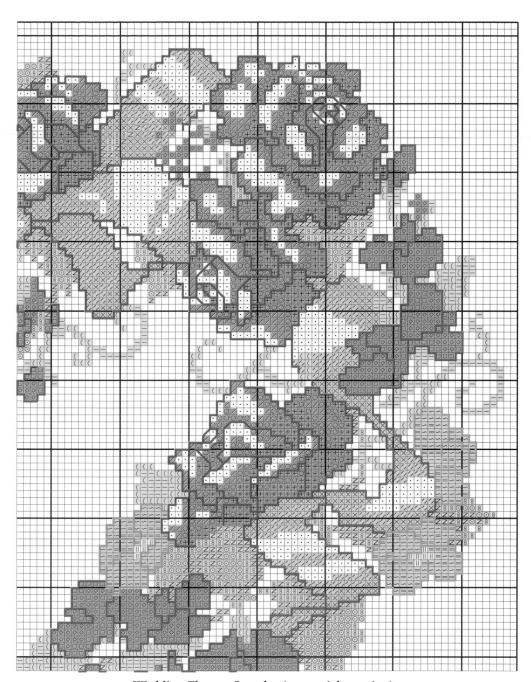

Wedding Flowers Sampler (upper right section)

ANCHOR		DMC	COLOR	
293	‖	727	Vy. Lt. Topaz	
2	·	WHITE	White and Kreinik 095 Starburst	
			BACKSTITCH (use 1 strand except where indicated)	
131	∟	798	Dk. Delft	Ribbon
33	∟	892	Med. Carnation	Sweet pea
161	∟	826	Med. Blue	Blue flowers; Lettering, 2 strands

ANCHOR		DMC	COLOR	
68	∟	3687	Mauve	Roses; Heart on picture frame, 2 strands
49	∟	3689	Lt. Mauve	Double heart on name section, 2 strands
878	∟	502	Blue-Green	Stems
130	∟	809	Delft	Border, 2 strands

Overlap from adjacent section ↗

Wedding Flowers Sampler (lower left section)

Overlap
from
adjacent
section

Wedding Flowers Sampler (lower right section)

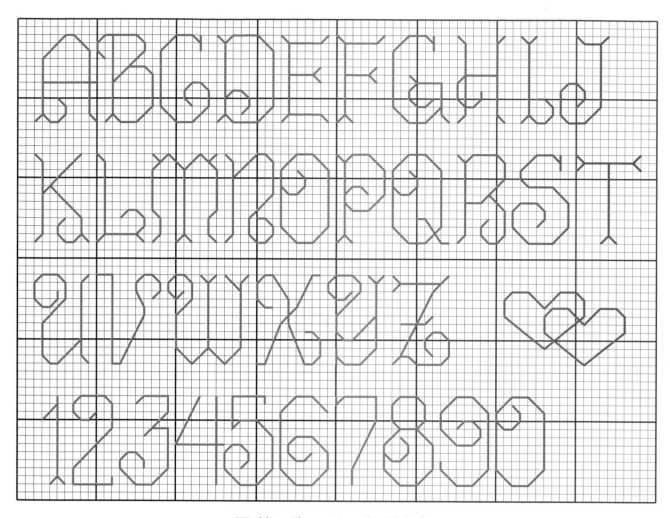

Wedding Flowers Sampler Alphabet

Bride's Handkerchief
♥

Materials

Stitched over 14-count waste canvas. The waste canvas was cut 4" x 4" inches. The finished design size, including initials, is 2½" x 2½".

● White fine cotton or linen lady's handkerchief with lace edging

continued

Stitch

Place the waste canvas diagonally across one corner of the handkerchief; baste in place. Find and mark the center of the canvas. Using the rose from the side motif of the frame chart, line up the center of the motif with the center of the canvas. Work one rose. To work the initials, turn the chart so that the vertical and horizontal stitching lines of the initial become diagonal, and the diagonal stitching lines become vertical and horizontal. Leave two threads between the rose and the nearest line of each chosen initial. Work cross-stitch over one thread. Use two strands of floss to work the cross-stitch and one strand for the backstitch. Follow the cross-stitch instructions given in Cross-Stitch Basics.

Finish

Trim excess canvas. Dampen the canvas and gently pull the threads, one at a time, to remove.

Alternate Design Sizes	
Stitches Per Inch	Design Sizes
11	3¼" x 1¾"
14	2½" x 1¼"
18	2" x 1"
22	1½ " x ¾"

Heart Charm

♥

Chart shown below

Materials

Stitched over two threads on 28-count White Quaker Cloth (Zweigart #3993, #100). The fabric was cut 4" x 4". Finished charm size is 3" x 2¾".

- Fusible interfacing: 4" x 4"
- Medium heart charm, 2½"x 2½" (Pat and Pam)
- White satin rattail, ⅛" diameter: 10"

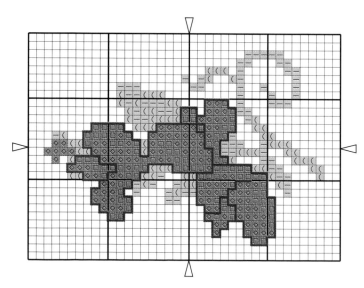

Wedding Flowers Heart Charm

- White satin ribbon, ⅛" wide: 24"
- Transfer paper

Stitch

Find and mark the center of the fabric. Line up the center of the outlined section of the sampler chart with the center of the fabric. Follow the cross-stitch instructions given in Cross-Stitch Basics.

Finish

Following manufacturer's instructions, fuse the interfacing to the back of the cross-stitched front piece. Keeping the design centered, transfer the heart shape to the cross-stitched piece and cut out. Following manufacturer's instructions, secure this piece to the charm. Glue the rattail around the edges beginning and ending at the center top. Cut a piece of ribbon 6 inches long. Thread through the hanging loop of the charm and tie the ends in a knot to secure. Cut the remaining ribbon in half and, holding the pieces together, tie a bow. Glue to top front of the heart over the raw ends of the rattail.

Alternate Design Sizes	
Stitches Per Inch	Design Sizes
11	3" x 2"
14	2½" x 1¾"
18	1¾" x 1¼"
22	1½" x 1"

Floral Border Frame
♥
Chart on page 76

Materials

Stitched over two threads on 28-count White Quaker Cloth (Zweigart #3993, #100). The fabric was cut 11" x 13". Finished frame size is 8½" x 11".

- Fusible interfacing: 11" x 13"
- Foam core board: 8½" x 11" with a 4½" x 7" opening for picture
- Cardboard for frame backing
- Fabric for frame backing
- White felt: 9" x 12"
- White rope-twist braid piping, ¼" diameter: 48"
- Craft glue
- Fray Check™

Stitch

At the upper left corner of the fabric, measure and mark a point 1½ inches in from each edge. Begin stitching the outer corner of the border chart at this point. Repeat the side motif four times across the top and bottom edges of the frame and six times along the side edges, rotating the chart at each corner as shown in the photograph. Follow the cross-stitch instructions given in Cross-Stitch Basics.

continued

Finish

Following manufacturer's instructions, fuse the interfacing to the back of the cross-stitched piece. Trim this piece to 1½ inches outside the stitching all around. Cut the felt to the same dimensions as the foam core. Glue the felt over the foam core. Position the cross-stitched piece over the felt side of the foam core; hold in place with pins. Pull the excess fabric at each side to the back of the foam core and glue in place. Remove pins. Allow the glue to dry thoroughly. Mark a line all around center opening 1½ inches inside the stitching. Cut out along the marked lines, cutting a diagonal slash toward each corner (see Diagram) to aid in turning fabric to back of frame. Pull the excess fabric through the center opening to the back of the foam core and glue in place. Dab each corner with Fray Check™ to prevent fraying. Allow to dry. Position the braid piping around the outer edge of the frame. Using the cardboard and backing fabric, follow the instructions on page 215 to make the frame backing.

Alternate Design Sizes	
Stitches Per Inch	Design Sizes
11	9¾" x 13"
14	7¾" x 10"
18	6" x 7¾"
22	5" x 6½"

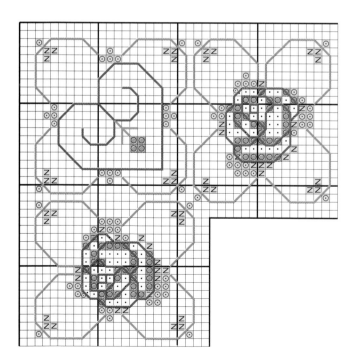

Wedding Flowers Floral Border Frame

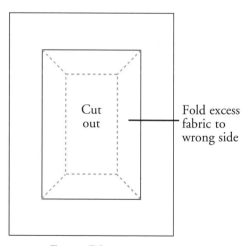

Cut out

Fold excess fabric to wrong side

Frame Diagram

Ring Bearer's Pillow

♥

Materials

Stitched over two threads on 28-count White Quaker Cloth (Zweigart #3993, #100). The fabric was cut 13" x 13". Finished pillow size is 10½" x 10½", excluding ruffle.

continued

- White fabric for pillow back: 13" x 13"
- Fusible interfacing: 13" x 13"
- Pregathered white lace edging, 1½" wide: 48"
- Pregathered white lace edging with pearls, ¾" wide: 48"
- Light pink jacquard ribbon, ½" wide: 24"
- Light pink picot-edged satin ribbon, ¼" wide: 1 yard
- White satin ribbon, ⅜" wide: 2 yards
- White satin ribbon, ⅛" wide: 2 yards
- Polyester stuffing
- Sewing thread to match fabric

Stitch

In the lower left corner of the Quaker Cloth, baste a 4 inch x 4½ inch area, approximately 1½ inches in from edges. Find and mark the center of the thread-marked area. Line up the center of the rose section on the left hand side of the sampler chart with the center of the marked area. Use two strands of the floss to work the cross-stitch design and one strand to work backstitch. Work cross-stitch over two threads. Follow the cross-stitch instructions given in Cross-Stitch Basics.

Finish

Following manufacturer's instructions, fuse the interfacing to the wrong side of the cross-stitched pillow top. Cut both the top and back 11½ x 11½ inches square. Cut the light pink jacquard ribbon in half. Position ribbon pieces on the pillow top, approximately 3 inches in from two adjacent sides, so that they crisscross in the corner opposite the cross-stitched design; tack in place (see Diagram, opposite). With right sides together, pin the pillow top and back together. Taking a ½-inch seam, stitch around three sides and four corners, leaving an opening for turning. Grade seam allowances, trim corners, and turn right side out. Stuff, then slipstitch the opening closed.

Cut gathered lace edgings to fit around pillow, adding 1 inch for joining. With right sides up and gathered edges aligned, place lace with pearls on top of other lace; sew gathered edges together. Sew the short ends of the doubled lace together to form a ring, finishing ends neatly. Sew around the outer edges of the pillow. Cut a 24-inch piece from the ⅛-inch ribbon. Fold in half and tack at the fold to the center of the pillow top for tying the ring(s). Cut pink picot-edged ribbon in half. Hold these pieces together with remaining white ⅛-inch ribbon, and the ⅜-inch ribbon. Tack ribbons together in the center, then tack to pillow top 1 inch above the cross-stitched design. Tie bows as desired, allowing ends to form streamers.

Alternate Design Sizes	
Stitches Per Inch	Design Sizes
11	5" x 5"
14	4" x 4½"
18	3" x 3"
22	2½" x 2½"

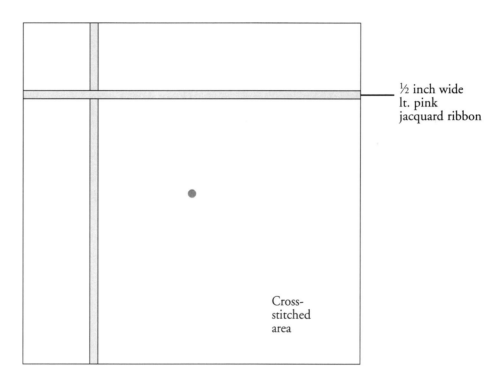

½ inch wide
lt. pink
jacquard ribbon

Cross-stitched area

Ring Bearer's Pillow

Rose Garden

By all means, do promise yourself a rose garden—and then create a rosy haven in your home—a pretty corner, perhaps, filled with rose-patterned stitchery.

♥

You might begin with a romantic Rose Pillow, with its ribbon-tied bouquet of blossoms and delicate border. These elements provide countless possibilities for derivative projects. We've used the border to create a versatile square Table Scarf. A single rose in full bloom graces a Faux-Finish Box, and a freshly plucked bud from the main motif adorns the Rosebud Sachet. Filled with a sweetly scented rose potpourri, it will bring the scent of June into your "rose room" all year long.

Rose Pillow

♥

Chart on pages 84-87

Materials

Stitched over two threads on 28-count Cream Glasgow Linen (Zweigart #3685, #222). The fabric was cut 15" x 15". Finished pillow size is 14" x 14".

- Fabric for pillow back: ½ yard
- Peach twisted rope cording, ¾" in diameter: 1¾ yards
- Pillow form: 14" square (or polyester stuffing)
- Fray Check™
- Sewing thread to match fabric

Stitch

Find and mark the center of the fabric. Line up the center of the chart with the center of the fabric. Follow the cross-stitch instructions given in Cross-Stitch Basics.

Finish

Cut the pillow back fabric to the same dimensions as the cross-stitched pillow top. With right sides together, pin the top to the back. Stitch around 3 sides and 4 corners, taking a ½-inch seam, and leaving an opening for turning and stuffing. Grade seam allowances, trim corners, and turn right side

out. Insert pillow form or polyester stuffing. Slipstitch the opening closed. Sew the braid around the edges of the pillow, lapping and joining the ends. Dab the ends of the braid with Fray Check™ to prevent fraying.

Alternate Design Sizes	
Stitches Per Inch	Design Sizes
11	14¼" x 14¼"
14	11¼" x 11¼"
18	8¾" x 8¾"
22	7¼" x 7¼"

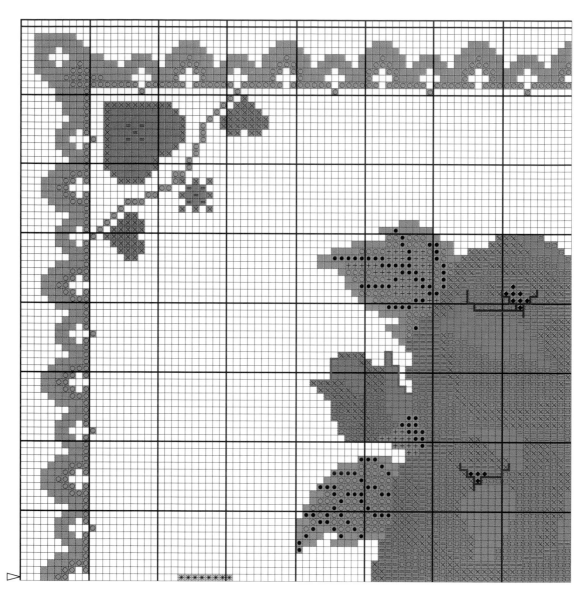

Rose Garden Pillow (upper left section)

ROSE GARDEN KEY

Note: *Use 1 skein of all floss colors except DMC #3348, which requires 2. Cross-stitch using 1 strand floss for Sachet, 2 strands for all other projects.*

ANCHOR		DMC	COLOR
271		819	Lt. Baby Pink
1021	□	761	Lt. Salmon
1022	✕	760	Salmon
1024	=	3328	Dk. Salmon
1005	◆	816	Garnet
928		3761	Vy. Lt. Sky Blue

ANCHOR		DMC	COLOR
129	·	3325	Lt. Baby Blue
1033	/	932	Lt. Antique Blue
1034	✳	931	Med. Antique Blue
264		3348	Lt. Yellow Green
860	○	522	Fern Green
262	+	3363	Med. Pine Green
862	●	520	Dk. Fern Green

BACKSTITCH (Use 1 strand)			
1005	⌐	816	Garnet
1022	⌐	760	Salmon

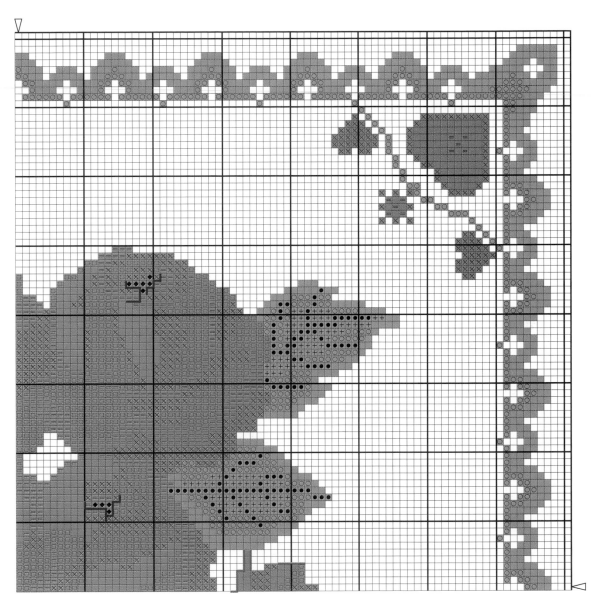

Rose Garden Pillow (upper right section)

Overlap from adjacent section →

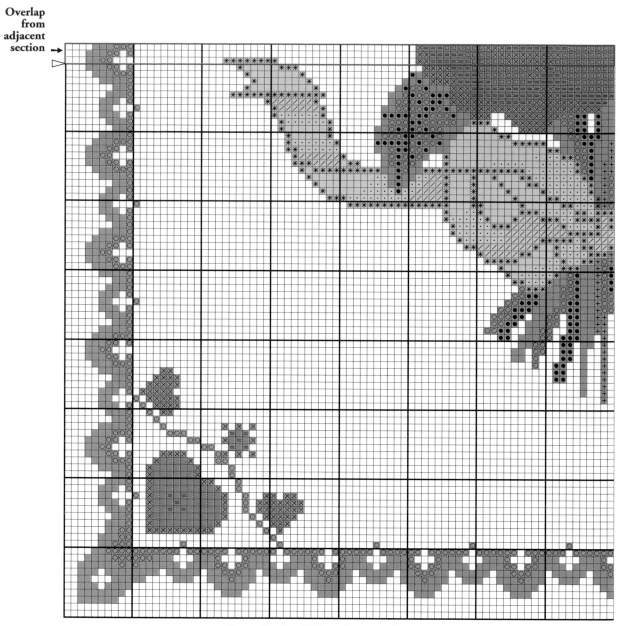

Rose Garden Pillow (lower left section)

ROSE GARDEN KEY

Note: *Use 1 skein of all floss colors except DMC #3348, which requires 2. Cross-stitch using 1 strand floss for Sachet, 2 strands for all other projects.*

ANCHOR		DMC	COLOR
271		819	Lt. Baby Pink
1021	□	761	Lt. Salmon
1022	×	760	Salmon
1024	=	3328	Dk. Salmon
1005	◆	816	Garnet
928		3761	Vy. Lt. Sky Blue

ANCHOR		DMC	COLOR
129	·	3325	Lt. Baby Blue
1033	/	932	Lt. Antique Blue
1034	✳	931	Med. Antique Blue
264		3348	Lt. Yellow Green
860	○	522	Fern Green
262	+	3363	Med. Pine Green
862	●	520	Dk. Fern Green

	BACKSTITCH (Use 1 strand)		
1005	⌐	816	Garnet
1022	⌐	760	Salmon

Overlap
from
adjacent
◄— section
◁

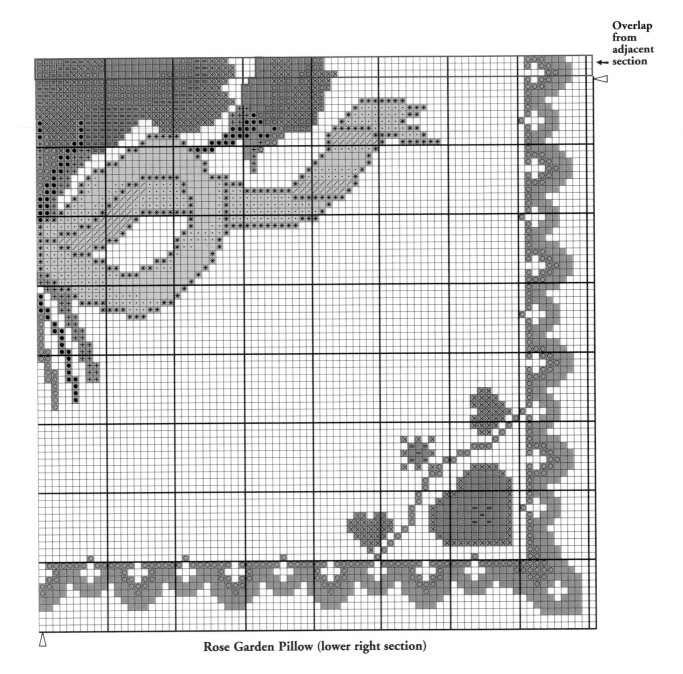

Rose Garden Pillow (lower right section)

Table Scarf
♥
Materials
Stitched over two threads on 28-count Cream Glasgow Linen (Zweigart #3685, #222). The fabric was cut 17" x 17". Finished scarf size is 15½" x 15½".

Stitch
Find and mark the center of the fabric. Use the border from the pillow chart. Line up the center of the chart with the center of the fabric. Follow the cross-stitch instructions given in Cross-Stitch Basics.

Finish
Staystitch 1½ inches from edges all around. Unravel threads to the stitching for fringe.

Alternate Design Sizes	
Stitches Per Inch	Design Sizes
11	14¼" x 14¼"
14	11¼" x 11¼"
18	8¾" x 8¾"
22	7¼" x 7¼"

Rosebud Sachet

♥

Chart shown below

Materials

Stitched on 18-count Cream Aida (Zweigart #3793, #264). The fabric was cut 7" x 16". Finished sachet bag size is 5" x 7", excluding the lace.

● Cream Cluny-type lace, 1" wide: 12"
● Decorative ribbon, ⅜" wide: 1 yard
● Potpourri
● Sewing thread to match fabric

Stitch

Fold the fabric in half crosswise. Find and mark the center of one half. Line up the center of the chart with the center of the marked fabric. Follow the cross-stitch instructions given in Cross-Stitch Basics.

Finish

Cut lace in half. With right sides up, lap straight edge of lace over short edge of cross-stitched fabric at each end. Stitch in place. With right sides together, fold fabric in half, bringing lace edges together. Stitch the side edges together, including ends of lace, taking ½-inch seams and leaving lace edge (top) open. Turn right side out. Fill with potpourri as desired and tie closed with the ribbon. Trim ends of ribbon.

Alternate Design Sizes	
Stitches Per Inch	Design Sizes
11	3" x 3½"
14	2¼" x 2¾"
18	1¾" x 2"
22	1½" x 1¾"

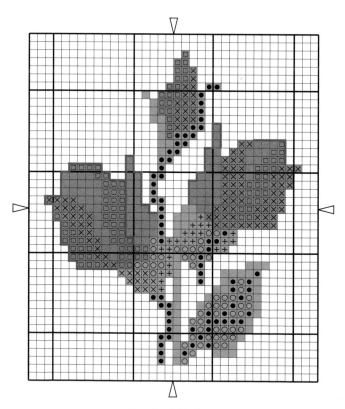

Rosebud Sachet

Faux-Finish Box
♥
Chart shown below

Materials

Stitched on 14-count Cream Aida (Zweigart #3706, #264). The fabric was cut 7" x 7". Finished box top size is 5" x 5".

● Faux-finish box, Malachite Green, 3" high x 6" wide x 6" deep (Sudberry House #9900)

Stitch

Find and mark the center of the fabric. Line up the center of the chart with the center of the fabric. Follow the cross-stitch instructions given in Cross-Stitch Basics.

Finish

Following the manufacturer's instructions, mount the fabric in the box top.

Alternate Design Sizes	
Stitches Per Inch	Design Sizes
11	4¾" x 4¼"
14	3¾" x 3¼"
18	3" x 2½"
22	2½" x 2"

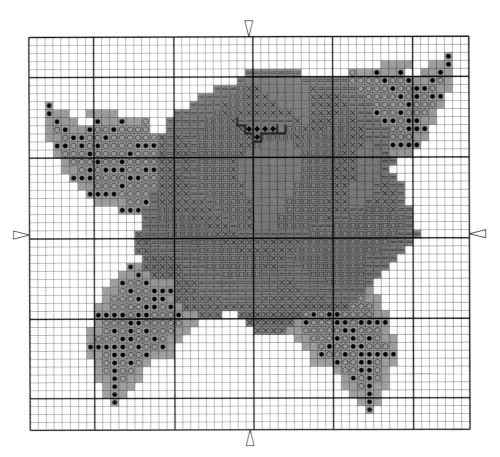

Rose Garden Faux-Finish Box

State Flowers

Do you know
what your state flower is?
It's fun to study this informative
poster-in-stitchery and
discover which bloom is symbolic
of your home state—or where
your favorite flower thrives.

♥

The spectacular State Flowers
Sampler is a tribute to the
American love of flowers and
natural beauty. Use your own
state flower (or another) as
a motif for a Cheeseboard, Tea
Towel, Potholder or Heart-
shaped Magnet—the design area
for each motif is the same
size. Any one of these projects
would make a great gift
for an out-of-state friend or
relative.

State Flowers Sampler

♥

Chart on pages 96-103

Materials
Stitched on 14-count Rustico (Zweigart #3953, #54). The fabric was cut 16¼" x 22¾". Finished size of framed sampler as shown is 14¼" x 20¾".

Stitch
Find and mark the center of the fabric. Line up the center of the chart with the center of the fabric. Follow the cross-stitch instructions given in Cross-Stitch Basics.

Finish
For best results, have this piece professionally matted and framed.

Alternate Design Sizes	
Stitches Per Inch	Design Sizes
11	16¾" x 25"
14	13¼" x 19½"
18	10¼" x 15¼"
22	8½" x 12½"

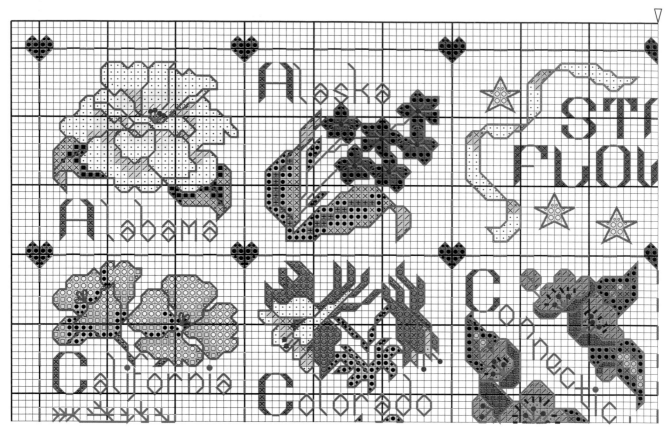

State Flowers Sampler (upper left section)

upper left	upper right
upper left center	upper right center
lower left center	lower right center
lower left	lower right

STATE FLOWERS KEY

Note: *Use 1 skein of all floss colors except DMC #322, White, #905, #471, #209, #726, and #347, which require 2, and #3799, which requires 3. Cross-stitch using 2 strands floss.*

ANCHOR		DMC	COLOR
271	·	819	Lt. Baby Pink
73	/	963	Ultra Vy. Lt. Dusty Rose
74	○	3354	Lt. Dusty Rose
76	✕	3731	Vy. Dk. Dusty Rose

ANCHOR		DMC	COLOR
59	+	326	Vy. Deep Rose
43	■	815	Med. Garnet
36	▢	3326	Lt. Rose
38	✕	335	Rose
11	●	350	Med. Coral
144	·	800	Pale Delft
136	/	799	Med. Delft
978	✕	322	Vy. Lt. Navy Blue
131	●	798	Dk. Delft
118	○	340	Med. Blue Violet
1030	✕	3746	Dk. Blue Violet
108	▢	210	Med. Lavender
109	+	209	Dk. Lavender
98	✕	553	Violet
102	●	550	Vy. Dk. Violet
275	·	746	Off White
293	/	727	Vy. Lt. Topaz
295	○	726	Lt. Topaz
303	▢	742	Lt. Tangerine
304	✕	741	Med. Tangerine
1025	●	347	Vy. Dk. Salmon
891	·	676	Lt. Old Gold
307	/	783	Med. Topaz
890	○	729	Med. Old Gold

State Flowers Sampler (upper right section)

ANCHOR		DMC	COLOR
309	×	781	Vy. Dk. Topaz
310	+	434	Lt. Brown
359	■	801	Dk. Coffee Brown
259	·	772	Vy. Lt. Yellow Green
253	/	472	Ultra Lt. Avocado Green
266	○	471	Vy. Lt. Avocado Green
256	×	704	Bright Chartreuse
257	●	905	Dk. Parrot Green
215	○	320	Med. Pistachio
267	×	469	Vy. Lt. Avocado Green
268	+	3345	Dk. Yellow Beige
269	●	936	Vy. Dk. Avocado Green
218	■	319	Vy. Dk. Pistachio
231	/	453	Lt. Shell Gray
233	×	451	Dk. Shell Gray
2	·	WHITE	White

BACKSTITCH

ANCHOR		DMC	COLOR
978	⌐	322	Vy. Lt. Navy Blue, 2 strands
268	⌐	3345	Dk. Hunter Green, 2 strands
236	⌐	3799	Vy. Dk. Pewter Gray, 1 strand
293		727	Vy. Lt. Topaz

FRENCH KNOTS (strands/wrap)

ANCHOR		DMC	COLOR
359	●	801	Dk. Coffee Brown (2/2)
304	●	741	Med. Tangerine (2/2)
295	●	726	Lt. Topaz (2/2)
978	●	322	Vy. Lt. Navy Blue (2/2)
293	●	727	Vy. Lt. Topaz (2/2)
891	●	676	Lt. Old Gold (2/2)
266	●	471	Vy. Lt. Avocado (2/2)
303	●	742	Lt. Tangerine (2/2)
236	○	3799	Vy. Dk. Pewter Gray (2/2)
295	○	726	Lt. Topaz (3/1)
303	○	742	Lt. Tangerine (3/1)

STRAIGHT STITCH (Use 2 strands)

ANCHOR		DMC	COLOR
309	\	781	Vy. Dk. Topaz
295	\	726	Lt. Topaz
1025	\	347	Vy. Dk. Salmon
303	/	742	Lt. Tangerine
268	\	3345	Dk. Hunter Green

RUNNING STITCH (Use 3 strands)

ANCHOR		DMC	COLOR
144	—	800	Pale Delft

LAZY DAISY STITCH (Use 2 strands)

ANCHOR		DMC	COLOR
253	Ɓ	472	Ultra Lt. Avocado
236	Ɓ	3799	Vy. Dk. Pewter Gray

↓ **Overlap from adjacent section**

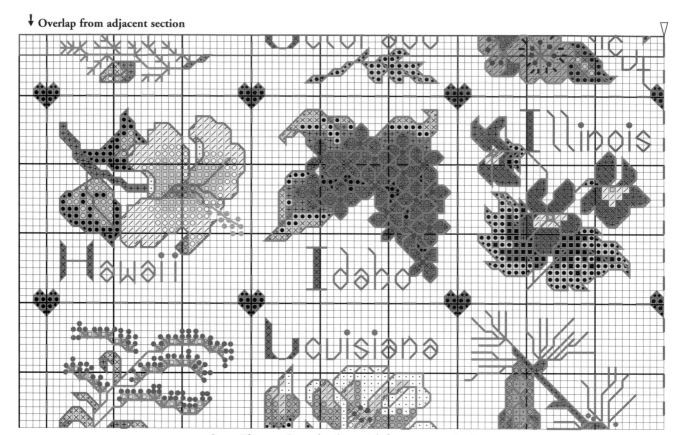

State Flowers Sampler (upper left center section)

upper left	upper right
upper left center	upper right center
lower left center	lower right center
lower left	lower right

STATE FLOWERS KEY

Note: *Use 1 skein of all floss colors except DMC #322, White, #905, #471, #209, #726, and #347, which require 2, and #3799, which requires 3. Cross-stitch using 2 strands floss.*

ANCHOR		DMC	COLOR
271	·	819	Lt. Baby Pink
73	/	963	Ultra Vy. Lt. Dusty Rose
74	O	3354	Lt. Dusty Rose
76	X	3731	Vy. Dk. Dusty Rose

ANCHOR		DMC	COLOR
59	+	326	Vy. Deep Rose
43	■	815	Med. Garnet
36	□	3326	Lt. Rose
38	X	335	Rose
11	●	350	Med. Coral
144	·	800	Pale Delft
136	/	799	Med. Delft
978	X	322	Vy. Lt. Navy Blue
131	●	798	Dk. Delft
118	O	340	Med. Blue Violet
1030	X	3746	Dk. Blue Violet
108	□	210	Med. Lavender
109	+	209	Dk. Lavender
98	X	553	Violet
102	●	550	Vy. Dk. Violet
275	·	746	Off White
293	/	727	Vy. Lt. Topaz
295	O	726	Lt. Topaz
303	□	742	Lt. Tangerine
304	X	741	Med. Tangerine
1025	●	347	Vy. Dk. Salmon
891	·	676	Lt. Old Gold
307	/	783	Med. Topaz
890	O	729	Med. Old Gold

Overlap from adjacent section ↓

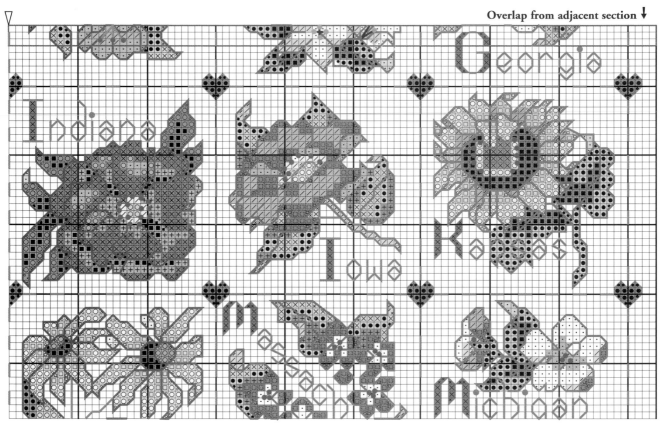

State Flowers Sampler (upper right center section)

ANCHOR		DMC	COLOR
309	✕	781	Vy. Dk. Topaz
310	+	434	Lt. Brown
359	■	801	Dk. Coffee Brown
259	·	772	Vy. Lt. Yellow Green
253	/	472	Ultra Lt. Avocado Green
266	○	471	Vy. Lt. Avocado Green
256	✕	704	Bright Chartreuse
257	●	905	Dk. Parrot Green
215	○	320	Med. Pistachio
267	✕	469	Vy. Lt. Avocado Green
268	+	3345	Dk. Yellow Beige
269	●	936	Vy. Dk. Avocado Green
218	■	319	Vy. Dk. Pistachio
231	/	453	Lt. Shell Gray
233	✕	451	Dk. Shell Gray
2	·	WHITE	White

		BACKSTITCH	
978	⌐	322	Vy. Lt. Navy Blue, 2 strands
268	⌐	3345	Dk. Hunter Green, 2 strands
236	⌐	3799	Vy. Dk. Pewter Gray, 1 strand
293		727	Vy. Lt. Topaz

ANCHOR		DMC	COLOR
		FRENCH KNOTS (strands/wrap)	
359	●	801	Dk. Coffee Brown (2/2)
304	●	741	Med. Tangerine (2/2)
295	●	726	Lt. Topaz (2/2)
978	●	322	Vy. Lt. Navy Blue (2/2)
293		727	Vy. Lt. Topaz (2/2)
891	●	676	Lt. Old Gold (2/2)
266	●	471	Vy. Lt. Avocado (2/2)
303	●	742	Lt. Tangerine (2/2)
236	○	3799	Vy. Dk. Pewter Gray (2/2)
295	○	726	Lt. Topaz (3/1)
303	○	742	Lt. Tangerine (3/1)
		STRAIGHT STITCH (Use 2 strands)	
309	\	781	Vy. Dk. Topaz
295	\	726	Lt. Topaz
1025	\	347	Vy. Dk. Salmon
303	\	742	Lt. Tangerine
268	\	3345	Dk. Hunter Green
		RUNNING STITCH (Use 3 strands)	
144	—	800	Pale Delft
		LAZY DAISY STITCH (Use 2 strands)	
253	Ꭷ	472	Ultra Lt. Avocado
236	Ꭷ	3799	Vy. Dk. Pewter Gray

↓ **Overlap from adjacent section**

State Flowers Sampler (lower left center section)

upper left	upper right
upper left center	upper right center
lower left center	lower right center
lower left	lower right

State Flowers Sampler (lower right center section)

↓ **Overlap from adjacent section**

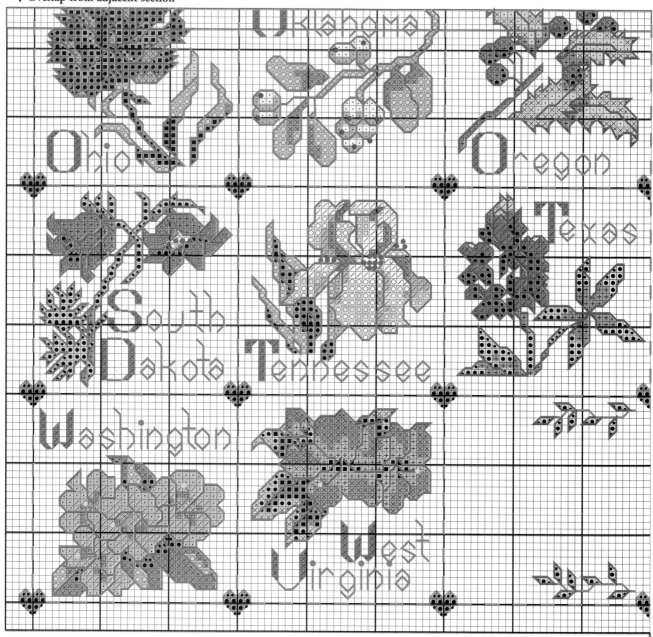

State Flowers Sampler (lower left section)

upper left	upper right
upper left center	upper right center
lower left center	lower right center
lower left	lower right

Overlap from adjacent section ↓

State Flowers Sampler (lower right section)

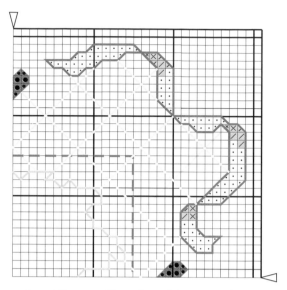

State Flowers Cheeseboard (quarter chart)

Cheeseboard

♥

Chart shown above

Materials
Stitched on 14-count Rustico (Zweigart #3953, #54). The fabric was cut 7" x 7". Finished stitched cheeseboard size is 5" x 5".

● Cutting board, 8" x 15" (Sudberry House #95299)

Stitch
NOTE: Each flower chart area is 30 squares x 30 squares.

Find and mark the center of the fabric. Line up the quarter chart with the upper right quarter of the fabric. Rotate the quarter chart to complete the border. For the center motif, line up the upper right quarter of the desired flower from the Sampler chart with the green dashed line on the quarter chart. Follow the cross-stitch instructions given in Cross-Stitch Basics. When the cross-stitching is complete, work the back-stitch lattice as shown. Work from the edges toward the center, as the flower you have chosen will not necessarily have the same shape as the flower shown in the photograph.

Finish
Following manufacturer's instructions, mount the cross-stitched piece in the cutting board.

Alternate Design Sizes	
Stitches Per Inch	Design Sizes
11	5¾" x 5¾"
14	4½" x 4½"
18	3½" x 3½"
22	2¾" x 2¾"

Heart-shaped Magnet
♥

Materials

Stitched on 14-count Rustico (Zweigart #3953, #54). The fabric was cut 6" x 5". Finished magnet size is 4" x 3".

.

● Acrylic Heart magnet, 4" x 3"

Stitch

NOTE: Each flower chart area is 30 squares x 30 squares.

Find and mark the center of the fabric. Line up the center of the desired flower motif with the center of the fabric, omitting state name. Follow the cross-stitch instructions given in Cross-Stitch Basics.

Finish

Trim the fabric ½ inch larger all around than the heart magnet. Following manufacturer's instructions, mount the cross-stitched piece in the magnet.

Alternate Design Sizes	
Stitches Per Inch	Design Sizes
11	2¼" x 2¼"
14	1¾" x 1¾"
18	1½" x 1½"
22	1" x 1"

Tea Towel

♥

Materials

Stitched on white tea towel with a 14-count insert (Charles Craft #TT-6626-6750). The tea towel is 16" x 26".

Stitch

NOTE: Each flower chart area is 30 squares x 30 squares.

Find and mark the center of the 14-count insert. Line up the center of the desired motif from the sampler chart with the center of the insert, omitting the state name; stitch that flower first. Then arrange and stitch a flower on either side of the center one, as desired, spacing motifs about ½-¾ inch apart. Follow the cross-stitch instructions given in Cross-Stitch Basics. Stitch 1 row of cross-stitch across the 11th row down from the top and across the 11th row up from the bottom or as desired; use a color of floss to complement your flowers.

Finish

The tea towel requires no finishing.

Alternate Design Sizes	
Stitches Per Inch	Design Sizes
11	7" x 2¼"
14	5½" x 1¾"
18	4" x 1½"
22	3½" x 1"

Potholder

♥

Materials

Stitched on a white quilted potholder with a 14-count insert (Charles Craft #PH-6200). The potholder is 8" x 8".

Stitch

NOTE: Each flower chart area is 30 squares x 30 squares.

Find and mark the center of the insert on the potholder. Line up the center of the desired flower motif from the sampler chart, omitting the state name, with the center of the fabric. Follow the cross-stitch instructions given in Cross-Stitch Basics. Work 1 row of cross-stitch across the 17th row from the top edge, or as desired; choose a color of floss to complement your flower.

Finish

The potholder requires no finishing.

Alternate Design Sizes	
Stitches Per Inch	Design Sizes
11	2¼" x 2¼"
14	1¾" x 1¾"
18	1½" x 2½"
22	1" x 1"

Flower Garden

A formal flower garden is the focal point of a timeless, traditional Flower Garden Sampler. It has all the elements of a classic American sampler—a Bible verse, a variety of motifs, and lots of color, texture and charm. The geometric lines of the stately home and its garden at the center of the sampler are nicely offset by the whimsical quality of its floral borders.

♥

Motifs from the sampler are repeated in clever and graphic ways for the accompanying projects—the Flower Frame, Shaker Box, Garden Box Insert and Tea Towel.

Flower Garden Sampler

♥

Chart on pages 112-115

Materials
Stitched on 14-count Summer Khaki Aida (Zweigart #3706, #323). The fabric was cut 14" x 18". Finished size of framed sampler as shown is 12½" x 16¼".

Stitch
Find and mark the center of the fabric. Line up the center of the chart with the center of the fabric. Stitching with 3 strands of floss, follow the cross-stitch instructions given in Cross-Stitch Basics.

Finish
For best results, have this piece professionally matted and framed.

Alternate Design Sizes	
Stitches Per Inch	Design Sizes
11	12¾" x 17¾"
14	10" x 14"
18	8" x 10¾"
22	6½" x 9"

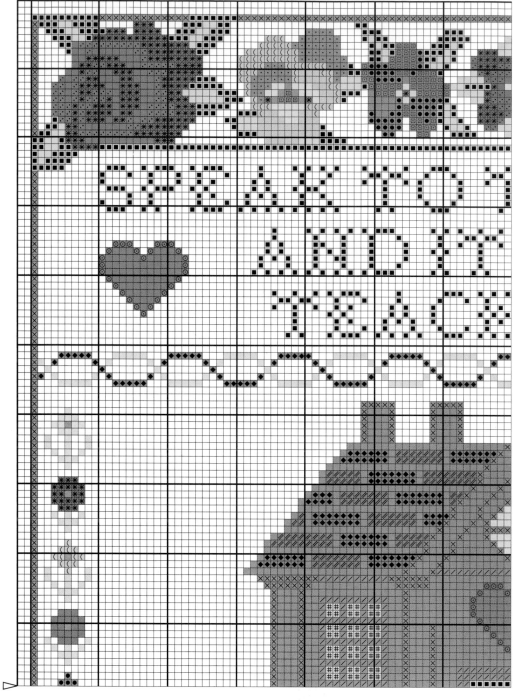

Flower Garden Sampler (upper left section)

FLOWER GARDEN KEY

Note: *Use 1 skein of all floss colors except Ecru and DMC #918, which require 3, and #319, which requires 2. The number of strands of floss used is given in the directions for each project. Note: #894 is used only on the picture frame, and #502 only on the Garden Box insert.*

ANCHOR		DMC	COLOR
1020		3713	Vy. Lt. Salmon
9	.·	352	Lt. Coral
10	⊙	351	Coral
42	✳	309	Deep Rose
27	○	894	Vy. Lt. Carnation
342		211	Lt. Lavender
870	·	3042	Lt. Antique Violet
119	⊡	333	Vy. Dk. Blue Violet

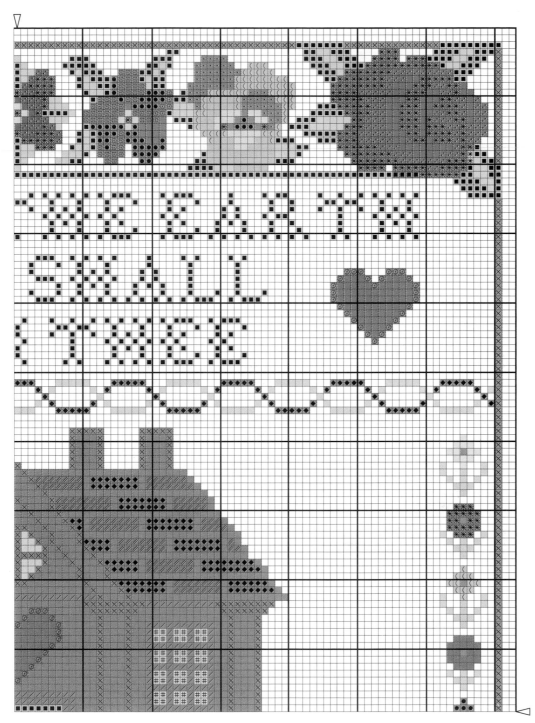

Flower Garden Sampler (upper right section)

ANCHOR		DMC	COLOR	ANCHOR		DMC	COLOR
100	●	327	Vy. Dk. Violet	832	╱	612	Med. Drab Brown
160		827	Vy. Lt. Blue	898	✕	611	Dk. Drab Brown
978	⟮	322	Vy. Lt. Navy Blue	215		320	Med. Pistachio
882		758	Vy. Lt. Terra Cotta	218	■	319	Vy. Dk. Pistachio
1013	╱╱	3778	Lt. Terra Cotta	877	〰	502	Blue Green
341	◆	918	Dk. Red Copper	1043	☐	369	Vy. Lt. Pistachio
305		725	Topaz	398		415	Pearl Gray
387		ECRU	Ecru	235	#	414	Dk. Steel Gray

Overlap from adjacent section →

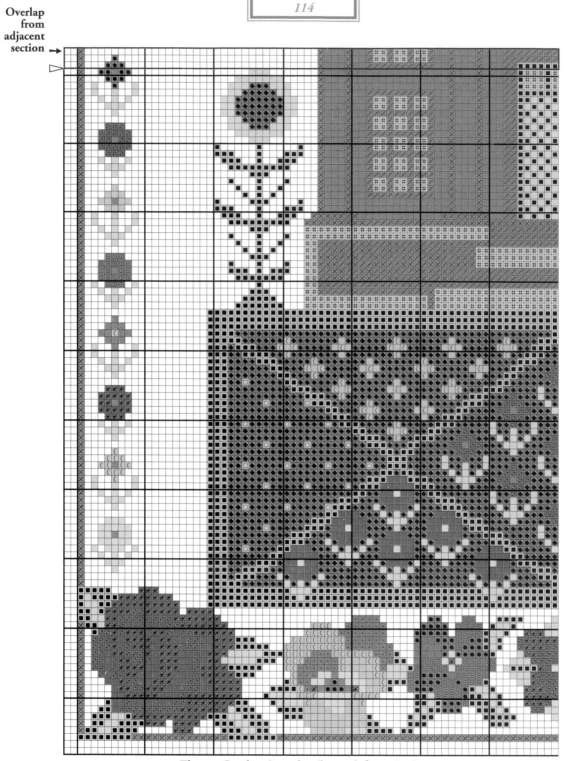

Flower Garden Sampler (lower left section)

FLOWER GARDEN KEY

Note: *Use 1 skein of all floss colors except Ecru and DMC #918, which require 3, and #319, which requires 2. The number of strands of floss used is given in the directions for each project. Note: #894 is used only on the picture frame, and #502 only on the Garden Box insert.*

ANCHOR		DMC	COLOR
1020		3713	Vy. Lt. Salmon
9		352	Lt. Coral
10		351	Coral
42		309	Deep Rose
27		894	Vy. Lt. Carnation
342		211	Lt. Lavender
870		3042	Lt. Antique Violet
119		333	Vy. Dk. Blue Violet

Overlap from adjacent section

Flower Garden Sampler (lower right section)

ANCHOR		DMC	COLOR	ANCHOR		DMC	COLOR
100	●	327	Vy. Dk. Violet	832	/	612	Med. Drab Brown
160		827	Vy. Lt. Blue	898	✕	611	Dk. Drab Brown
978	(	322	Vy. Lt. Navy Blue	215		320	Med. Pistachio
882		758	Vy. Lt. Terra Cotta	218	■	319	Vy. Dk. Pistachio
1013	//	3778	Lt. Terra Cotta	877	~	502	Blue Green
341	◆	918	Dk. Red Copper	1043	□	369	Vy. Lt. Pistachio
305		725	Topaz	398		415	Pearl Gray
387		ECRU	Ecru	235	#	414	Dk. Steel Gray

Flower Frame

♥

Chart shown below

Materials

Stitched on 14-count Summer Khaki Aida (Zweigart #3706, #323). The fabric was cut 12" x 10". Finished size is 10" x 8".

- Foam core board: 10" x 8" inches with a 6 ½" x 4½" opening for picture
- Cardboard for frame backing
- Beige felt
- Fabric for frame backing
- Craft glue
- Fray Check™

Stitch

Chart shown is for upper left hand corner. To complete frame as shown, baste a 6½-inch-wide by 4½-inch-high rectangle centered on the fabric. Position inner corner of chart at upper left hand corner of basted rectangle. Stitching with 3 strands of floss and varying colors of flowers in a random manner, follow the cross-stitch instructions given in Cross-Stitch Basics. Following the pattern sequence illustrated, work 1 flower in each corner, 8 along each side and 13 along the top and bottom edges.

Finish

Cut the felt to the same size and dimensions as the foam core. Glue the felt to the foam core. Keeping the design centered, position the embroidered piece over the felt-covered side of the foam core. Hold in place with pins. Pull the excess fabric at each edge to the back side of the foam core and glue in place; trim excess fabric at corners. Remove pins. Allow the glue to dry thoroughly. Mark a line 1½ inches inside the stitched design all around for the center opening. Cut out the marked rectangle. Clip the fabric diagonally into each corner, to aid in turning fabric to back of frame. Pull the excess fabric around the center opening to the back of the foam core and glue in place. Dab each corner with Fray Check™ to prevent fraying. Allow to dry. Using the cardboard and backing fabric, follow instructions on page 216 to make the frame backing.

Alternate Design Sizes	
Stitches Per Inch	Design Sizes
11	10¾" x 9"
14	8½" x 7"
18	6½" x 5½"
22	5½" x 4½"

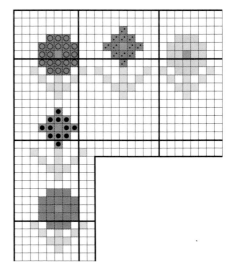

Flower Garden Frame

Tea Towel

♥

Materials

Stitched on tea towel with 14-count Aida insert (Charles Craft #HO6515-6750). The tea towel is 15" x 26".

Stitch

Find and mark the center of the 14-count insert on the tea towel. Line up the center of the center section of the large flower border from the sampler chart with the center of the insert. Stitching with 3 strands of floss, follow the cross-stitch instructions given in Cross-Stitch Basics.

Finish

The tea towel requires no finishing.

Alternate Design Sizes	
Stitches Per Inch	Design Sizes
11	7¾" x 1½"
14	6" x 1¼"
18	4¾" x 1"
22	4" x ¾"

Garden Box Insert

♥

Chart shown below

Materials

Stitched on 8-count Sage Hertarette (Zweigart #3707, #611). The fabric was cut 9" x 7". Finished box top size is 7" x 5".

● Rectangular box, 2½" high x 8" wide x 6" deep (Sudberry House #99701)

Stitch

Find and mark the center of the fabric. Line up the center of the chart with the center of the fabric. Stitching with all 6 strands of floss, follow the cross-stitch instructions given in Cross-Stitch Basics.

Finish

Following manufacturer's instructions, mount the fabric in the box top.

Alternate Design Sizes	
Stitches Per Inch	Design Sizes
8	7½" x 5¼"
11	5½" x 3¾"
14	4¼" x 3"
18	3½" x 2½"
22	2¾" x 2"

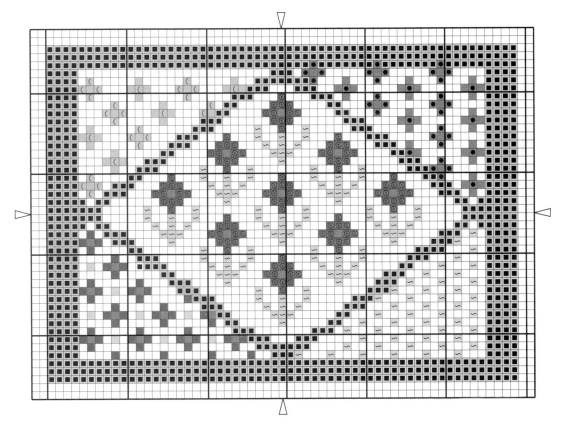

Flower Garden Box Insert

Shaker Box
♥
Chart shown below

Materials
Stitched on 8-count Off-White Hertarette (Zweigart #3707, #264). The fabric was cut 7" x 7". Finished box top size is 5½" in diameter.

- Shaker box, 3" high x 5½" in diameter (Sudberry House #9964)
- Batting

Stitch
Find and mark the center of the fabric. Line up the center of the chart with the center of the marked fabric. Stitching with all 6 strands of floss, follow the cross-stitch instructions given in Cross-Stitch Basics.

Finish
Keeping the design centered, trim the fabric and the batting to a circle 6 inches in diameter. Following manufacturer's instructions, mount the fabric over the batting in the top of the box.

Alternate Design Sizes	
Stitches Per Inch	Design Sizes
8	4½" x 5¼"
11	3¼" x 3¾"
14	2½" x 3"
18	2" x 2½"
22	1¾" x 2"

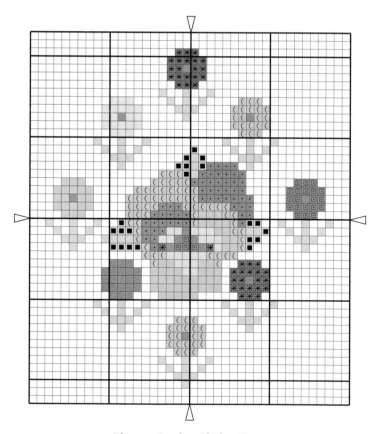

Flower Garden Shaker Box

Stylized Flowers

The artisans of
the Middle East and Far East
have long been masters
in the use of stylized flowers in
their woven and embroidered
textiles. Here, intricate floral and
heart motifs stand out against
a lush red background to create
a sophisticated design.

♥

The striking Table Runner
resembles a miniature Oriental
carpet. Motifs from the main
design have been adapted
to create a coordinating Candle
Screen, Bookmark and Glass
Heart Paperweight.

Table Runner

♥

Chart on pages 126-29

Materials

Stitched over two threads on 27-count Victorian Christmas Red Linda (Zweigart #1235, #906). The fabric was cut 17" x 35". Finished runner size is 17" x 35".

- Blue moiré fabric for backing: 19" x 37"
- Blue tassels, 4" long: 2
- Dressmaker's pencil
- Sewing thread to match fabric

Stitch

Find and mark the center of the fabric. Noting that chart shows only half the design, line up the center of the design with the center of the fabric. Work cross-stitch over two threads. Work chart in reverse for second half; do not repeat center row. Follow the cross-stitch instructions given in Cross-Stitch Basics.

Finish

Place the cross-stitched piece wrong side facing up. On each long edge, measure and mark 5½ inches in from each end; draw a line joining the corresponding markings on opposite edges to mark off a centered, rectangular area measuring 17 x 24 inches. Measure and mark the center of each short edge of embroidered piece. Draw lines from the center of each short edge to the corners of the marked rectangle to form a triangle at each end (see Diagram on page 130). Cut along the marked lines to shape the pointed ends of the table runner. Cut the moiré backing to the same shape, adding a 1 inch seam allowance all around. Turn edges of the backing up ½ inch; press, forming miters at corners. With wrong sides together, center the cross-stitched piece over the backing and pin in place. Fold the extending backing over the edges of the right side of the cross-stitched piece, forming a binding with mitered corners and points. Stitch in place. Sew a tassel to each point.

Alternate Design Sizes	
Stitches Per Inch	Design Sizes
11	13" x 18½"
14	10¼" x 14½"
18	8" x 11½"
22	6½" x 9¼"
27	10¾" x 15¼"

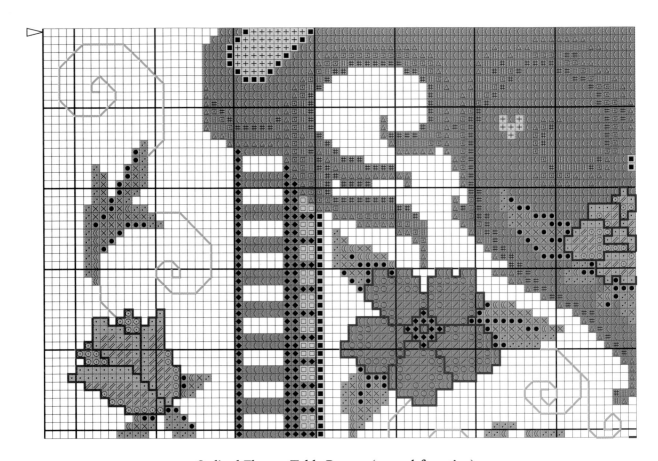

Stylized Flowers Table Runner (upper left section)

STYLIZED FLOWERS KEY

Note: *Use 1 skein of all floss colors except DMC #712, which requires 2. Cross-stitch using 1 strand floss for Paperweight, 2 strands for all other projects.*

Note: *White is used on the Candle Screen only.*

ANCHOR		DMC	COLOR
2		WHITE	White
1011		948	Vy. Lt. Peach Flesh
1012		754	Lt. Peach Flesh
1015	◆	3777	Vy. Dk. Terra Cotta
1033	□	932	Lt. Antique Blue
1034	+	931	Med. Antique Blue
150	■	336	Navy Blue
926		712	Cream

ANCHOR		DMC	COLOR
886	◣	677	Vy. Lt. Old Gold
891	‖	676	Lt. Old Gold
890	◨	729	Med. Old Gold
901	#	680	Dk. Old Gold
6	.	353	Peach Flesh
9	/	352	Lt. Coral
11	⊙	350	Med. Coral
859	▨	523	Lt. Fern Green
262	×	3052	Med. Green Gray
862	(((	520	Dk. Fern Green
683	●	500	Vy. Dk. Blue Green

BACKSTITCH (Use 1 strand)			
683	⌐	500 - vines	Vy. Dk. Blue Green
1015	⌐	3777 - flowers	Vy. Dk. Terra Cotta

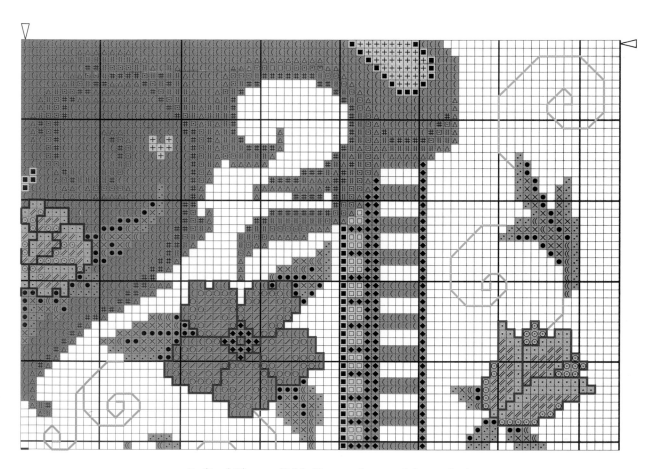

Stylized Flowers Table Runner (upper right section)

↓ **Overlap from adjacent section**

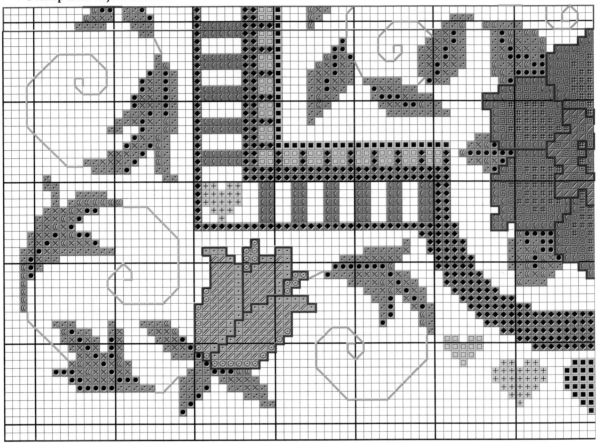

Stylized Flowers Table Runner (lower left section)

STYLIZED FLOWERS KEY

Note: *Use 1 skein of all floss colors except DMC #712, which requires 2. Cross-stitch using 1 strand floss for Paperweight, 2 strands for all other projects.*
Note: *White is used on the Candle Screen only.*

ANCHOR		DMC	COLOR
2	◡	WHITE	White
1011	◉	948	Vy. Lt. Peach Flesh
1012		754	Lt. Peach Flesh
1015	◆	3777	Vy. Dk. Terra Cotta
1033		932	Lt. Antique Blue
1034	+	931	Med. Antique Blue
150	■	336	Navy Blue
926		712	Cream

ANCHOR		DMC	COLOR
886	△	677	Vy. Lt. Old Gold
891	‖	676	Lt. Old Gold
890		729	Med. Old Gold
901	#	680	Dk. Old Gold
6	·	353	Peach Flesh
9	/	352	Lt. Coral
11	⊙	350	Med. Coral
859		523	Lt. Fern Green
262	✕	3052	Med. Green Gray
862		520	Dk. Fern Green
683	●	500	Vy. Dk. Blue Green

		BACKSTITCH (Use 1 strand)	
683	⌐	500 - vines	Vy. Dk. Blue Green
1015	⌐	3777 - flowers	Vy. Dk. Terra Cotta

Overlap from adjacent section ↓

Stylized Flowers Table Runner (lower right section)

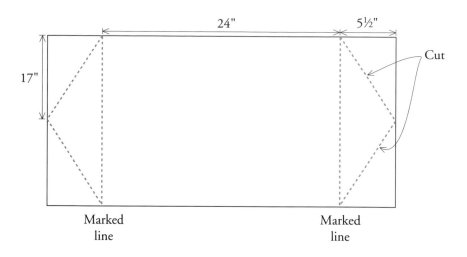

Table Runner

Bookmark
♥
Chart on page 133

Materials
Stitched over two threads on 27-count Victorian Christmas Red Linda (Zweigart #1235, #906). The fabric was cut 5" x 10". Finished bookmark size is 3" x 8".

● Thread to match fabric

Stitch
Find and mark the center of the fabric. Line up the center of the chart with the center of the fabric. Follow the cross-stitch instructions given in Cross-Stitch Basics.

Finish

Trim fabric to 3½" x 8½". Staystitch ¼ inch away from edges all around. Unravel the threads to the staystitching line.

Alternate Design Sizes	
Stitches Per Inch	Design Sizes
11	1¾" x 5"
14	1½" x 4"
18	1" x 3"
22	¾" x 2½"
27	1½" x 4"

Glass Heart Paperweight

♥

Chart on page 133

Materials

Stitched on 18-count Cream Aida (Zweigart #3793, #264). The fabric was cut 5" x 5". Finished paperweight size is 3½" x 3½".

● Heart-shaped glass paperweight 3½" x 3½" (Yarn Tree Designs)

Stitch

Find and mark the center of the fabric. Using the paperweight chart, line up the center of the rose motif with the center of the fabric. Follow the cross-stitch instructions given in Cross-Stitch Basics.

Finish

Trim fabric to fit inside the paperweight. Following manufacturer's instructions, mount the fabric in the paperweight.

Alternate Design Sizes	
Stitches Per Inch	Design Sizes
11	3¼" x 1¾"
14	2½" x 1¼"
18	2" x 1"
22	1½" x ¾"

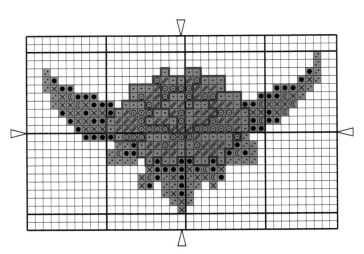

Stylized Flowers Paperweight

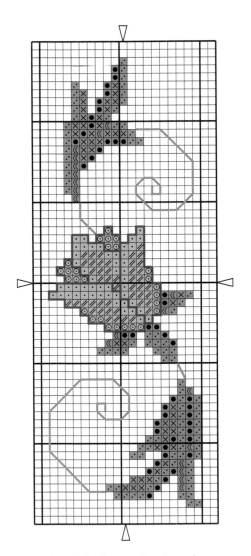

Stylized Flowers Bookmark

Candle Screen

♥

Chart on page 135

Materials

Stitched over two threads on 27-count Victorian Christmas Red Linda (Zweigart #1235, #906). The fabric was cut 6" x 8". Finished size is 5" x 7".

● Candle screen: Large, 6½"wide x 20½" tall (Sudberry House #21001)

Stitch

Find and mark the center of the fabric. Line up the center of the chart with the center of the fabric. Work cross-stitch over two threads. Follow the cross-stitch instructions given in Cross-Stitch Basics.

Finish

Following manufacturer's instructions, mount the fabric in the screen.

Alternate Design Sizes	
Stitches Per Inch	Design Sizes
11	5½" x 8¼"
14	4½" x 6½"
18	3½" x 5"
22	2¾" x 4"
27	4½" x 6¾"

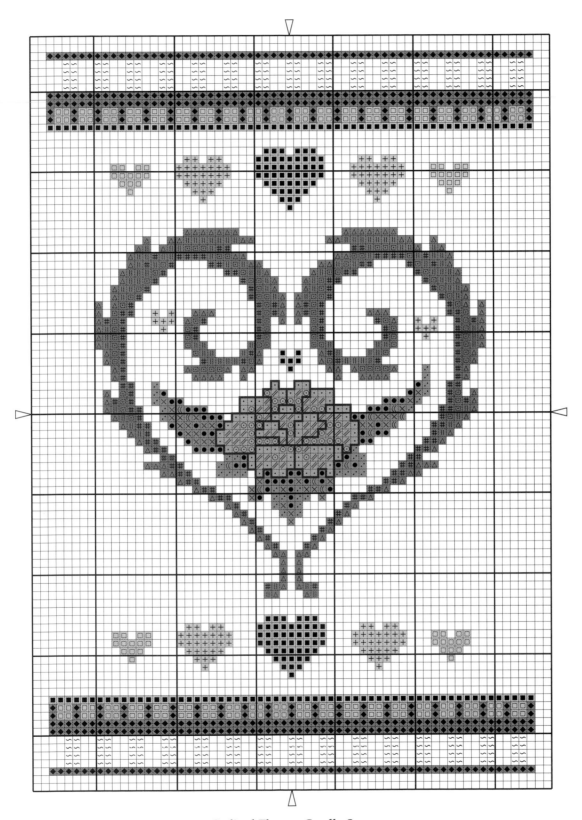

Stylized Flowers Candle Screen

Victorian Valentine

The Victorian era is synonymous with lavish decoration, exemplified by the generous use of hearts and flowers on just about everything. What, then, could be more romantic than a Victorian valentine?

♥

The colorfully beaded and stitched Heart Sampler features a "lace-trimmed" heart that stands out boldly against a black background. This and all of the other beautiful projects are of keepsake quality, to be treasured or given straight from the heart. Included are an elegant Beaded Bag, a silk Rose Camisole, a beaded Heart Pincushion, a Bookmark and a Cut-Glass Jewelry Jar.

Beaded Heart Sampler
♥
Chart on pages 140-43

Materials

Stitched on 14-count Black Aida 14 (Zweigart #3706, #95). The fabric was cut 13" x 15". Finished size of framed sampler as shown is 11" x 13".

- Beads: glass seed beads (Mill Hill Glass Beads), see the Key for colors
- Sewing thread to match fabric

Stitch

Find and mark the center of the fabric. Line up the center of the chart with the center of the fabric. Follow the instructions given for stitching with beads given in Cross-Stitch Basics.

Finish

For best results, have this piece professionally matted and framed.

Alternate Design Sizes	
Stitches Per Inch	Design Sizes
11	13½" x 10¾"
14	10¾" x 8½"
18	8½" x 6½"
22	6¾" x 5½"
To stitch with beads, you must use 14-count fabric	

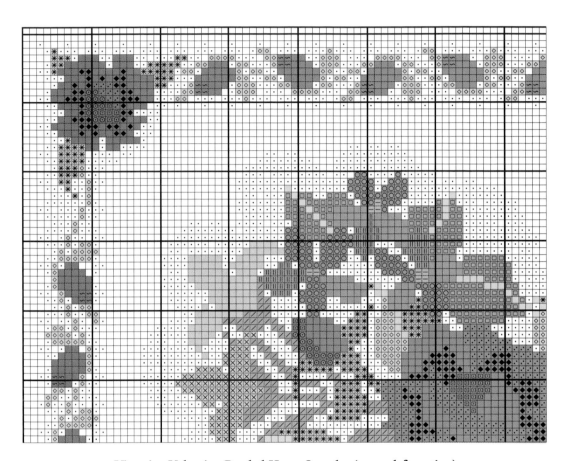

Victorian Valentine Beaded Heart Sampler (upper left section)

VICTORIAN VALENTINE KEY

Note: *Use 1 skein of all floss colors except White, which requires 3. Use 1 package of all beads except #62035, which requires 3, and #00128 and #00553, which require 2. Cross-stitch using 2 strands floss or the number of strands given in the directions for the project.*

Note: *Beads #62012 and #00020 are only used on the Heart Sampler.*

Key for Heart Sampler, Cut-Glass Jewelry Jar, Beaded Bag, and Heart Pincushion

ANCHOR		DMC	COLOR
46	+	666	Bright Christmas Red
9046	#	321	Christmas Red
63	⊡	602	Med. Cranberry
45	◆	814	Dk. Garnet
255	◇	907	Lt. Parrot Green
257	✳	905	Dk. Parrot Green
923	■	699	Christmas Green
209	□	912	Lt. Emerald Green
188	/	943	Med. Aquamarine
110	△	208	Vy. Dk. Lavender
89	//	917	Med. Plum
332	⅛	608	Bright Orange
304	−	741	Med. Tangerine
2	·	WHITE	White

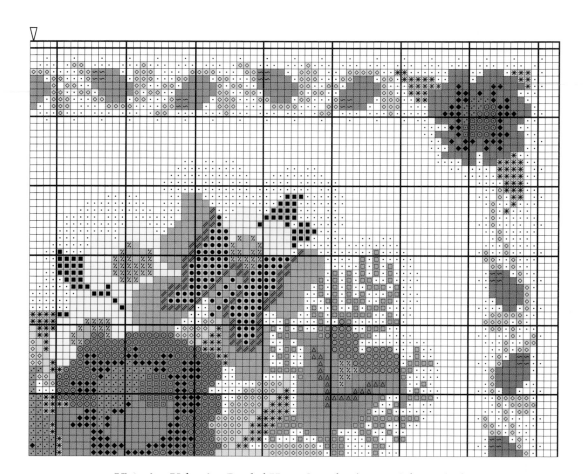

Victorian Valentine Beaded Heart Sampler (upper right section)

	BEADS	COLOR
	02003	Peach Cream
⟋	62036	Frosted Pink Coral
	62035	Frosted Peppermint
∴	00145	Pink
⊙	00553	Old Rose
⌣	62012	Frosted Gunmetal
	00332	Emerald
	02008	Sea Breeze
●	00020	Royal Blue
✕	02007	Satin Blue
	02006	Ice Blue
	02009	Ice Lilac
○	62047	Frosted Lavender
‖	62034	Frosted Blue Violet
	00968	Red
	00128	Yellow

↓ **Overlap from adjacent section**

Victorian Valentine Beaded Heart Sampler (lower left section)

VICTORIAN VALENTINE KEY

Note: *Use 1 skein of all floss colors except White, which requires 3. Use 1 package of all beads except #62035, which requires 3, and #00128 and #00553, which require 2. Cross-stitch using 2 strands floss or the number of strands given in the directions for the project.*

Note: *Beads #62012 and #00020 are only used on the Heart Sampler.*

Key for Heart Sampler, Cut-Glass Jewelry Jar, Beaded Bag, and Heart Pincushion

ANCHOR		DMC	COLOR
46	+	666	Bright Christmas Red
9046	#	321	Christmas Red
63	⊡	602	Med. Cranberry
45	◆	814	Dk. Garnet
255	◇	907	Lt. Parrot Green
257	✳	905	Dk. Parrot Green
923	■	699	Christmas Green
209	☐	912	Lt. Emerald Green
188	/	943	Med. Aquamarine
110	△	208	Vy. Dk. Lavender
89	⫽	917	Med. Plum
332	⁒	608	Bright Orange
304	—	741	Med. Tangerine
2	·	WHITE	White

Overlap from adjacent section ↓

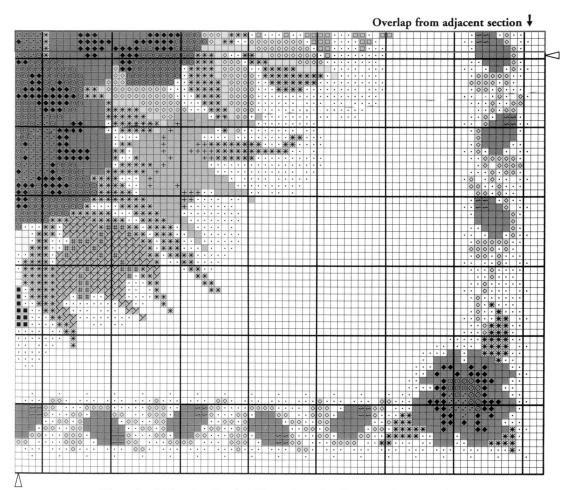

Victorian Valentine Beaded Heart Sampler (lower right section)

	BEADS	COLOR
	02003	Peach Cream
⟩	62036	Frosted Pink Coral
	62035	Frosted Peppermint
∴	00145	Pink
⊙	00553	Old Rose
~	62012	Frosted Gunmetal
	00332	Emerald
	02008	Sea Breeze
●	00020	Royal Blue
✕	02007	Satin Blue
	02006	Ice Blue
	02009	Ice Lilac
○	62047	Frosted Lavender
‖	62034	Frosted Blue Violet
	00968	Red
	00128	Yellow

Beaded Bag

♥

Chart on page 146

Materials

Stitched on 14-count Black Aida (Zweigart #3706, #95). The fabric was cut 7" x 16". Finished bag size is 5¼" x 7".

- Black fusible interfacing: 6½" x 16"
- Beads: glass seed beads (Mill Hill Glass Beads), see the Key for colors

- Matching thread
- Black beads for fringe: seed beads; 6mm and 15mm bugle beads (all from Westrim Crafts); 2 pebble beads (Mill Hill Glass Beads)
- Black round button, ½"
- Black rayon twisted rope cord, ½" in diameter: 1½ yards
- Black narrow elastic for button loop
- Sewing thread to match fabric

Stitch

Fold the Aida cloth in half crosswise. Center the chart on one half of the fabric, leaving 1 inch at the short edge unstitched. Follow the instructions for stitching with beads given in Cross-Stitch Basics.

Finish

Following manufacturer's instructions, fuse the interfacing to the wrong side of the cross-stitched fabric. Fold the fabric in half crosswise, wrong side out. Stitch the side edges together taking ½-inch seams; leave the top edge open. Turn right side out, fold the top edge ½ inch to the inside and slip-stitch in place. Sew button to the top edge at center front. Sew a loop of elastic, just long enough to loop over the button, to the opposite top edge. Finish the ends of the cord by wrapping tightly with thread. Sew ends of cord to inside of bag at top of seams.

Make the beaded fringe as follows, passing the thread through the beads as shown by the arrows in the illustrations: Never tie knots when beading; always start and finish by running the thread back through the completed beading. Cut a 1½-yard length of thread. Thread the needle and, working with a single thread, string 6 beads leaving a 4 inch tail. Continue as shown in Figure 1, sections A, B, and C, until you have a strip the width of the lower edge of the bag for header.

Attach a new thread by weaving through the header beads to one edge. String beads following the order shown in Figure 2. Pass the thread through the header as shown, then string a second strand of beads, adding two beads to the 5-bead section. Repeat in this manner, adding two beads to each strand until the middle of the header strip is

reached; repeat in reverse to the outer edge.

Sew the fringe to the lower edge of the bag by slipstitching through the loops between the top beads in the header.

Knot a double strand of thread securely around one pebble bead. Cover the pebble bead with alternating rows of 4 and 5 seed beads. Using the same thread, string 50 seed beads and form a loop. Secure to the covered pebble bead and repeat to complete the tassel. Make another tassel. Sew tassels to outside of bag at top of seams.

Alternate Design Sizes	
Stitches Per Inch	Design Sizes
11	7" x 9¼"
14	5½" x 7¼"
18	4½" x 5½"
22	3½" x 4½"

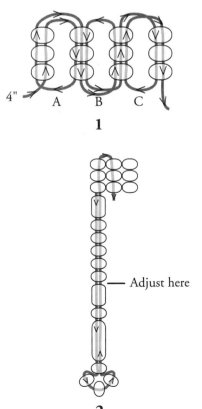

Beaded Fringe for Bag

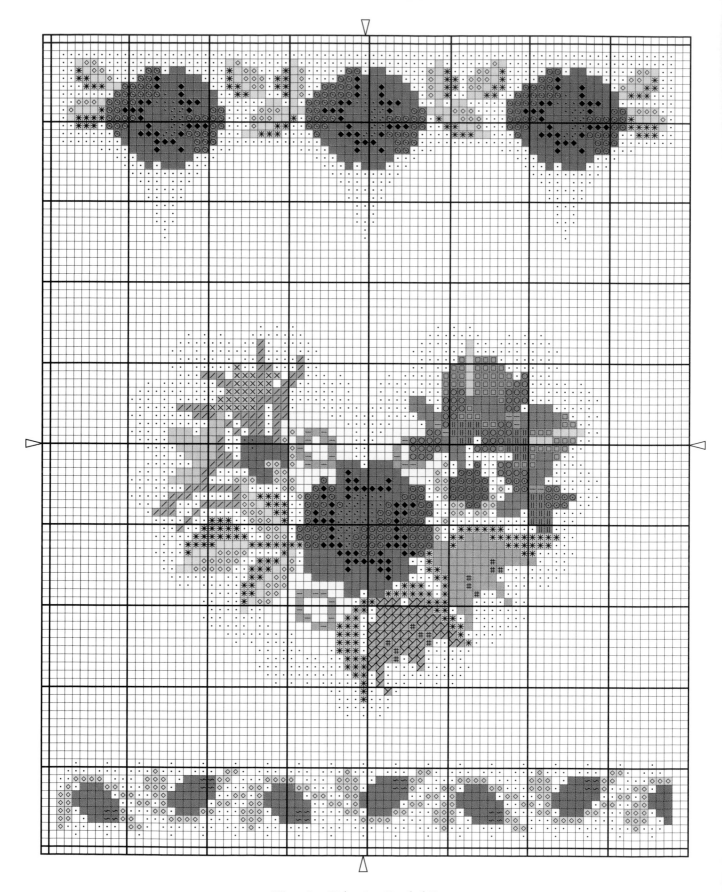

Victorian Valentine Beaded Bag

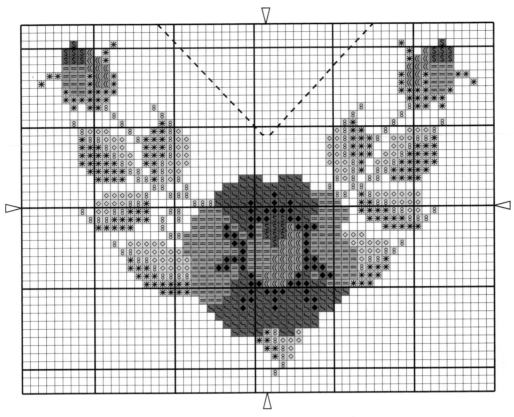

Victorian Valentine Rose Camisole

Rose Camisole
♥
Chart shown above

Materials

Stitched over 14-count waste canvas (Charles Craft). The waste canvas was cut 7" x 7".

● White silk camisole (Dharma Trading Co. #SCAM)

Stitch

First, to be sure the design fits at the neckline of your camisole, mark the design area onto the waste canvas. Then, position and baste the waste canvas in place at the center front of the camisole with the center of the motif starting ½ inch below the neckline.

The canvas will extend into the neckline. Find and mark the center of the canvas. Line up the center of the chart with the center of the canvas. Work the cross-stitch motif. Follow the cross-stitch instructions given in Cross-Stitch Basics.

Finish

Trim off excess canvas. Dampen the canvas and gently pull the threads to remove them completely.

Alternate Design Sizes	
Stitches Per Inch	Design Sizes
11	5 "x 4"
14	4" x 3"
18	3" x 2½"
22	2½" x 2"

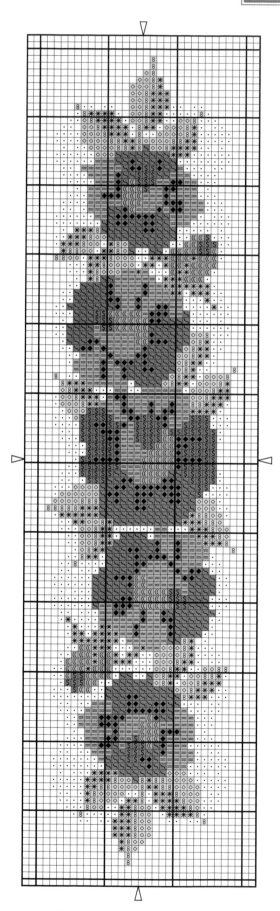

Victorian Valentine Bookmark

VICTORIAN VALENTINE CAMISOLE AND BOOKMARK KEY

Note: *Cross-stitch using 2 strands floss for Camisole and 1 strand floss for Bookmark.*

ANCHOR		DMC	COLOR
255	◇	907	Lt. Parrot Green
257	✳	905	Dk. Parrot Green
228	8	700	Bright Christmas Green
50	⦅	605	Vy. Lt. Cranberry
62	=	603	Cranberry
45	◆	814	Dk. Garnet
86	∫	3608	Vy. Lt. Plum
88	∫	718	Plum
2	·	WHITE	White

Bookmark

♥

Chart shown at left

Materials
Stitched on 18-count Black bookmark (Jeanette Crews Designs). Finished size of bookmark is 3¾" x 9".

Stitch
Find and mark the center of the fabric. Line up the center of the chart with the center of the fabric. Follow the cross-stitch instructions given in Cross-Stitch Basics.

Finish
The bookmark requires no finishing.

Alternate Design Sizes	
Stitches Per Inch	**Design Sizes**
11	2¾" x 10¾"
14	2¼" x 8½"
18	1½" x 6½"
22	1½" x 5½"

Heart Pincushion

♥

Chart on page 150

Materials

Stitched on 14-count Black Aida (Zweigart #3706, #95). The fabric was cut 8" x 16". Finished pincushion size is 5¼" x 5".

● Beads: glass seed beads (Mill Hill Glass Beads)
● Matching thread
● Black seed beads for edging (Westrim Crafts)
● Polyester stuffing
● Tracing paper
● Sewing thread to match fabric

continued

Stitch

Cut the fabric into two 8-inch squares. Find and mark the center of one square. Line up the center of the chart with the center of the fabric. Using three strands of floss, follow the instructions for stitching with beads given in Cross-Stitch Basics.

Finish

Using the dotted outline on the chart as a guide, make a heart-shaped pattern 6 1/4 inches wide at the widest point. Center pattern over cross-stitched design and cut out. From the other square cut a second heart for back. With right sides together sew the top and back together, taking a ½-inch seam and leaving a 2-inch opening for turning. Trim and notch seam allowances; turn right side out, and stuff. Slipstitch the opening closed.

Edging: Starting at the point of the heart, secure a double strand of thread by pulling knot to the inside of the heart. String the thread with 12 black beads. Backstitch on the seamline of the heart, making a ⅜-inch long loop. Continue to work loops of beads along the edge of the heart, keeping the loops even and overlapping all loops in the

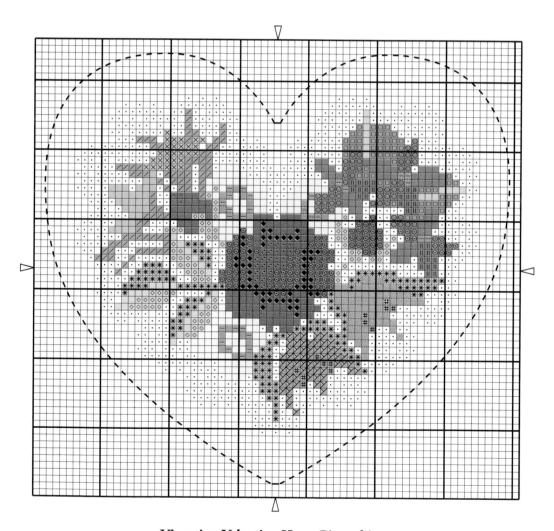

Victorian Valentine Heart Pincushion

same direction, until you reach the top of the heart; fasten securely. In the same manner, work edging from point to top along the opposite side of the heart.

Alternate Design Sizes	
Stitches Per Inch	Design Sizes
11	5½" x 4½"
14	4¼" x 3½"
18	3¼" x 2¾"
22	2¾" x 2¼"

Cut-Glass Jewelry Jar
♥
Chart shown below

Materials
Stitched on 14-count Black Aida (Zweigart #3706, #95). The fabric was cut 5" x 5". Finished jar top size is 3½" in diameter.

● Cut-glass jar (Anne Brinkley Designs CT 4)

Stitch
Find and mark the center of the fabric. Line up the center of the chart with the center of the fabric. Using three strands of floss, follow the instructions for stitching with beads given in Cross-Stitch Basics.

Finish
Keeping the design centered, trim the fabric to a circle 4 inches in diameter. Following manufacturer's instructions, mount the fabric in the jar lid.

Alternate Design Sizes	
Stitches Per Inch	Design Sizes
11	3¾" x 3¾"
14	3" x 3"
18	2¼" x 2¼"
22	2" x 2"

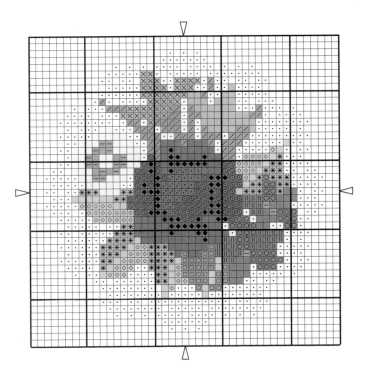

Victorian Valentine Jewelry Jar

Botanical Flowers

ased on technical drawings from the flower books and herbals of the 16th and 17th centuries, botanicals are a rich source of floral images. Here, four favorite flowers form a quartet of stitched botanical "prints" —Iris, Pansy, Cyclamen and Tiger Lily.

♥

Decorative borders are just right for variations on the theme. The four borders from the "prints" are arranged in parallel bands on a charming Tea Tray. The Iris border frames the face of the square Clock—though any of the other borders would be equally attractive. Likewise for the main flower designs; to adorn a small Pillow (or sachet), we picked the pansies. Note Cards make handsome use of the classic lettering that identifies each "print."

TIGER LILY

Botanical Print Samplers
(Tiger Lily, Iris, Pansy, Cyclamen)

♥

Charts on pages 156-71

Materials

Each sampler was stitched on 14-count Cream Aida (Zweigart #3706, #264). The fabric was cut 12¾" x 15". Finished size of framed sampler as shown is 10¾" x 13".

Stitch

Find and mark the center of the fabric. Line up the center of the appropriate chart with the center of the fabric. Follow the cross-stitch instructions given in Cross-Stitch Basics.

Finish

For best results, have this piece professionally matted and framed.

Alternate Design Sizes	
Stitches Per Inch	Design Sizes
11	10" x 12¾"
14	8" x 10"
18	6" x 7¾"
22	5" x 6½"

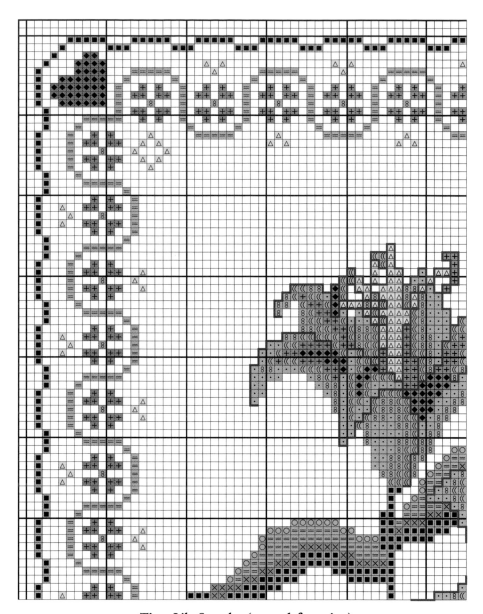

Tiger Lily Sampler (upper left section)

TIGER LILY KEY

Note: *Use 1 skein of all floss colors. Cross-stitch using 2 strands floss.*

ANCHOR		DMC	COLOR
1025	◆	347	Vy. Dk. Salmon
6	·	353	Peach Flesh
9	8	352	Lt. Coral
1003	⟨⟨	922	Lt. Copper
1042	○	504	Lt. Blue Green

ANCHOR		DMC	COLOR
215	=	320	Med. Pistachio
218	■	319	Vy. Dk. Pistachio
845	✕	730	Vy. Dk. Olive
307	△	783	Med. Topaz
11	+	350	Med. Coral
341	‖	918	Dk. Red Copper
BACKSTITCH			
1025	⌐	347	Vy. Dk. Salmon

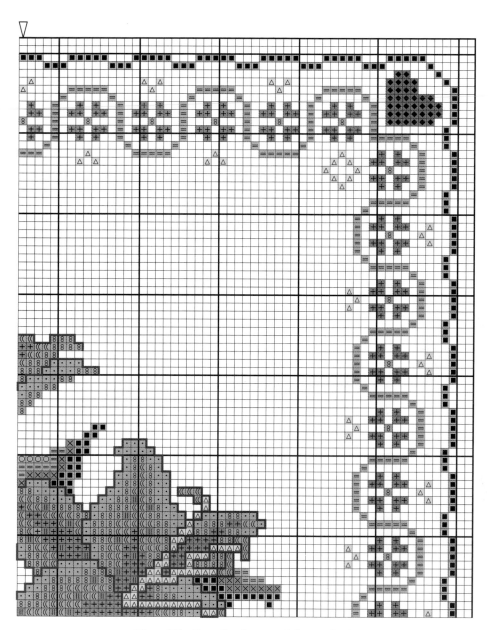

Tiger Lily Sampler (upper right section)

Overlap from adjacent section ➔

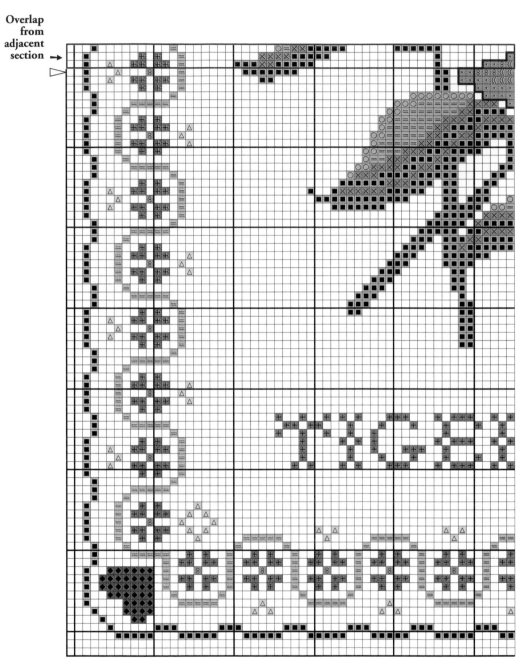

Tiger Lily Sampler (lower left section)

TIGER LILY KEY

Note: *Use 1 skein of all floss colors. Cross-stitch using 2 strands floss.*

ANCHOR		DMC	COLOR
1025	◆	347	Vy. Dk. Salmon
6	·	353	Peach Flesh
9	8	352	Lt. Coral
1003	((	922	Lt. Copper
1042	○	504	Lt. Blue Green

ANCHOR		DMC	COLOR
215	=	320	Med. Pistachio
218	■	319	Vy. Dk. Pistachio
845	✕	730	Vy. Dk. Olive
307	△	783	Med. Topaz
11	+	350	Med. Coral
341	‖	918	Dk. Red Copper
		BACKSTITCH	
1025	⌐	347	Vy. Dk. Salmon

Overlap from adjacent section

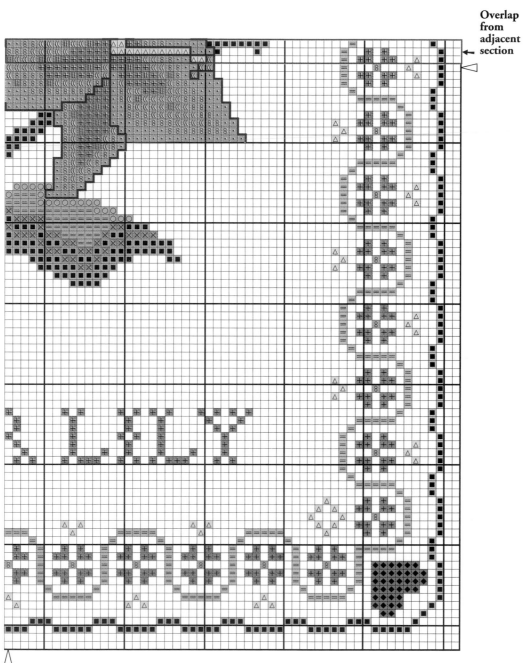

Tiger Lily Sampler (lower right section)

Iris Sampler (upper left section)

IRIS KEY

Note: *Use 1 skein of all floss colors. Cross-stitch using 2 strands floss.*

ANCHOR		DMC	COLOR
342	━	211	Lt. Lavender
109	∽	209	Dk. Lavender
110	Z	208	Vy. Dk. Lavender

ANCHOR		DMC	COLOR
100	✳	327	Vy. Dk. Violet
119	S	333	Vy. Dk. Blue Violet
144	□	800	Pale Delft
1042	○	504	Lt. Blue Green
215	═	320	Med. Pistachio
218	■	319	Vy. Dk. Pistachio

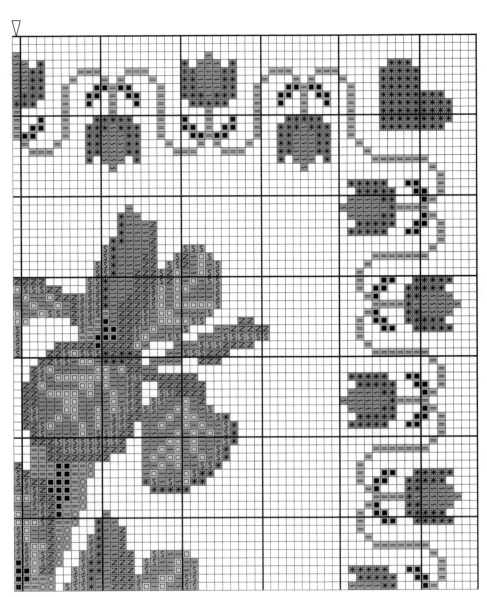

Iris Sampler (upper right section)

Overlap from adjacent section →

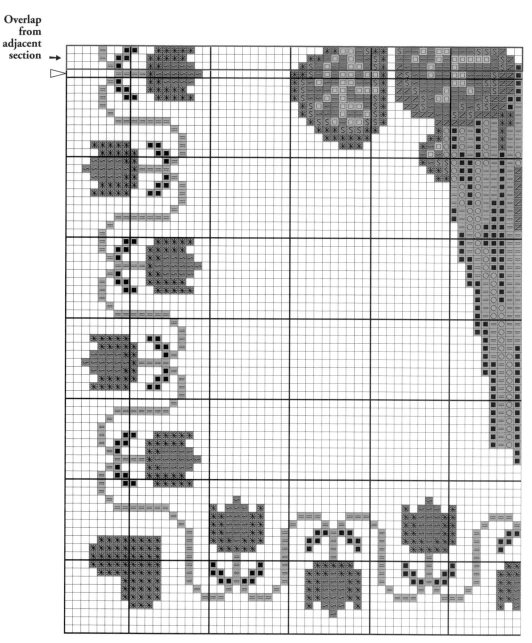

Iris Sampler (lower left section)

IRIS KEY

Note: Use 1 skein of all floss colors. Cross-stitch using 2 strands floss.

ANCHOR		DMC	COLOR
342	—	211	Lt. Lavender
109	∽	209	Dk. Lavender
110	Z	208	Vy. Dk. Lavender

ANCHOR		DMC	COLOR
100	✳	327	Vy. Dk. Violet
119	S	333	Vy. Dk. Blue Violet
144	□	800	Pale Delft
1042	○	504	Lt. Blue Green
215	=	320	Med. Pistachio
218	■	319	Vy. Dk. Pistachio

Overlap from adjacent section

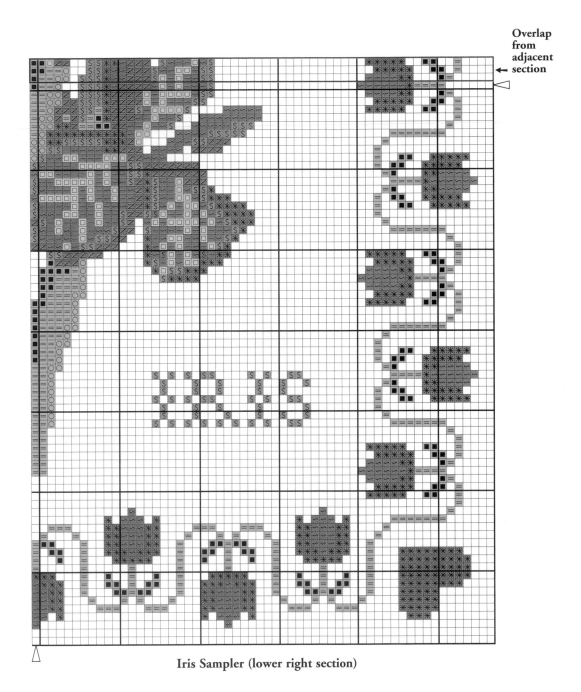

Iris Sampler (lower right section)

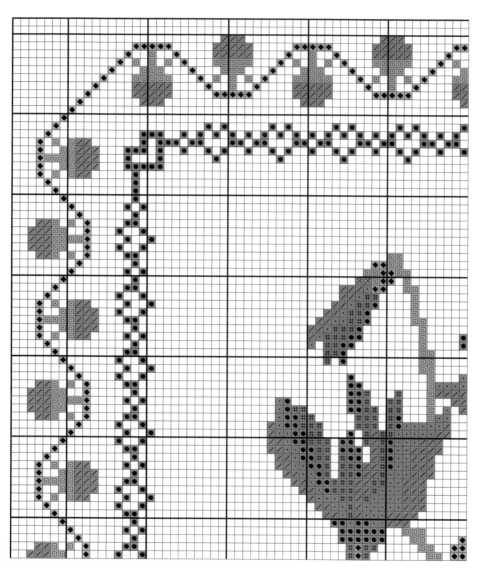

Cyclamen Sampler (upper left section)

CYCLAMEN KEY

Note: *Use 1 skein of all floss colors. Cross-stitch using 2 strands floss.*

ANCHOR		DMC	COLOR
1020	·	3713	Vy. Lt. Salmon
52	/	899	Med. Rose
42	#	309	Deep Rose
43	●	815	Med. Garnet

ANCHOR		DMC	COLOR
1042	◯	504	Lt. Blue Green
877	⊡	502	Blue Green
878	◆	501	Dk. Blue Green
845	✕	730	Vy. Dk. Olive

Cyclamen Sampler (upper right section)

Overlap from adjacent section →

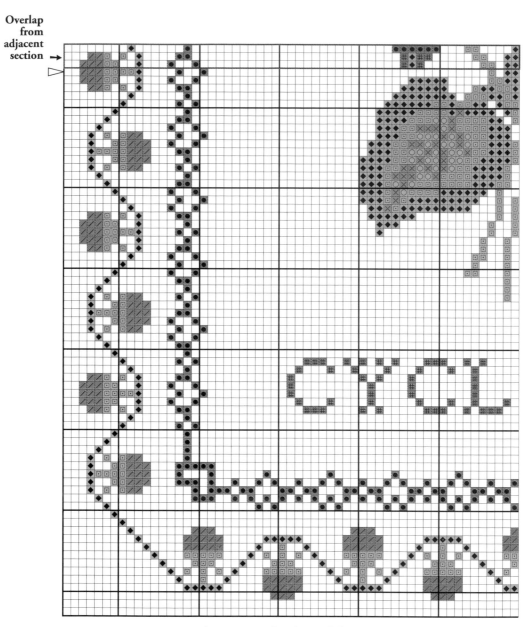

Cyclamen Sampler (lower left section)

CYCLAMEN KEY

Note: *Use 1 skein of all floss colors. Cross-stitch using 2 strands floss.*

ANCHOR		DMC	COLOR
1020	·	3713	Vy. Lt. Salmon
52	/	899	Med. Rose
42	#	309	Deep Rose
43	●	815	Med. Garnet

ANCHOR		DMC	COLOR
1042	○	504	Lt. Blue Green
877	·	502	Blue Green
878	◆	501	Dk. Blue Green
845	✕	730	Vy. Dk. Olive

Overlap from adjacent section

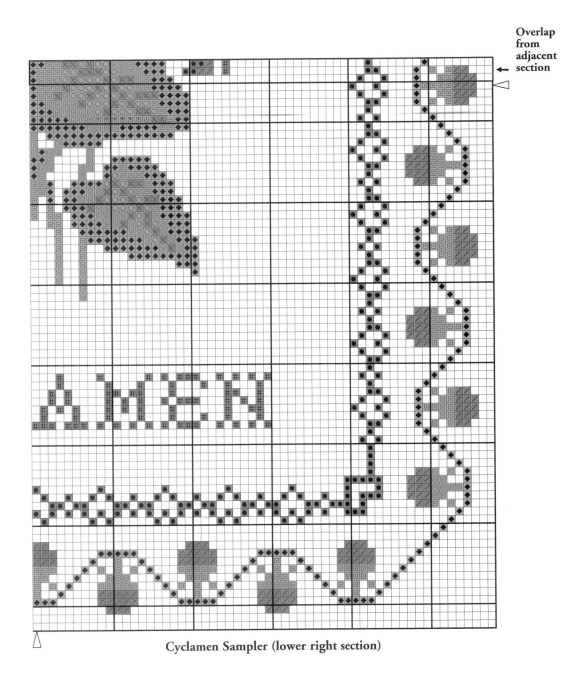

Cyclamen Sampler (lower right section)

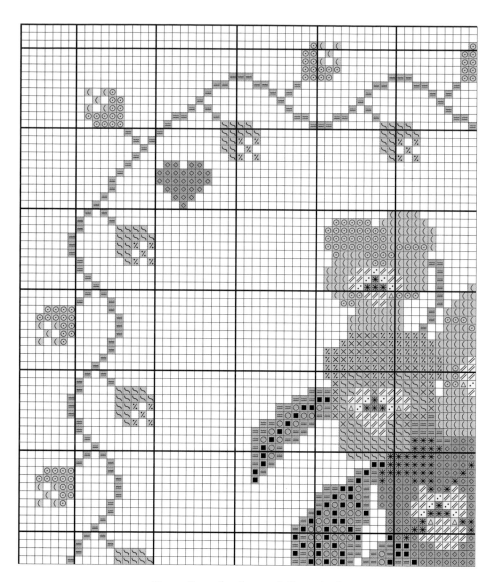

Pansy Sampler (upper left section)

PANSY KEY

Note: *Use 1 skein of all floss colors. Cross-stitch using 2 strands floss.*

ANCHOR		DMC	COLOR
24	◢	776	Med. Pink
40	✕	956	Geranium
59	⁒	326	Vy. Deep Rose
160	(	827	Vy. Lt. Blue
978	⊙	322	Vy. Lt. Navy Blue

ANCHOR		DMC	COLOR
1042	○	504	Lt. Blue Green
215	═	320	Med. Dk. Pistachio
218	■	319	Vy. Dk. Pistachio
307	△	783	Med. Topaz
387	·'	ECRU	Ecru
295	∥	726	Lt. Topaz
870	◇	3042	Lt. Antique Violet
100	✳	327	Vy. Dk. Violet

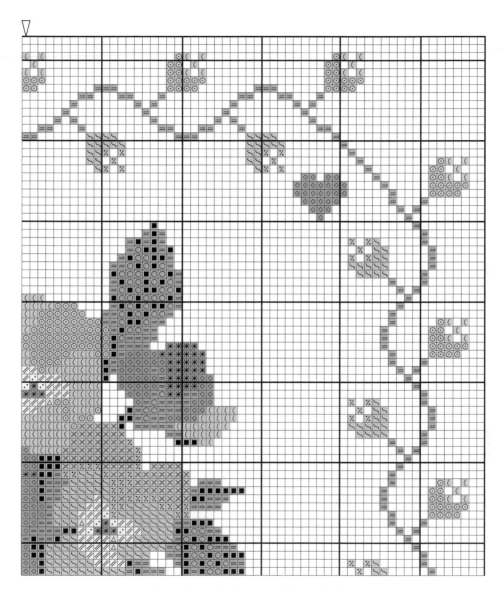

Pansy Sampler (upper right section)

**Overlap
from
adjacent
section** ➡

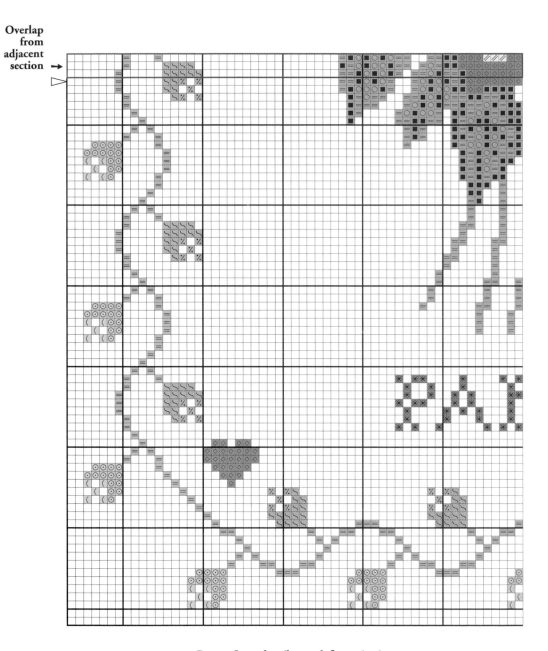

Pansy Sampler (lower left section)

PANSY KEY

Note: *Use 1 skein of all floss colors. Cross-stitch using 2 strands floss.*

ANCHOR		DMC	COLOR
24	◟	776	Med. Pink
40	✕	956	Geranium
59	⁒	326	Vy. Deep Rose
160	⟨	827	Vy. Lt. Blue
978	⊙	322	Vy. Lt. Navy Blue

ANCHOR		DMC	COLOR
1042	○	504	Lt. Blue Green
215	═	320	Med. Dk. Pistachio
218	■	319	Vy. Dk. Pistachio
307	△	783	Med. Topaz
387	∴	ECRU	Ecru
295	⫽	726	Lt. Topaz
870	◇	3042	Lt. Antique Violet
100	✳	327	Vy. Dk. Violet

Overlap from adjacent section

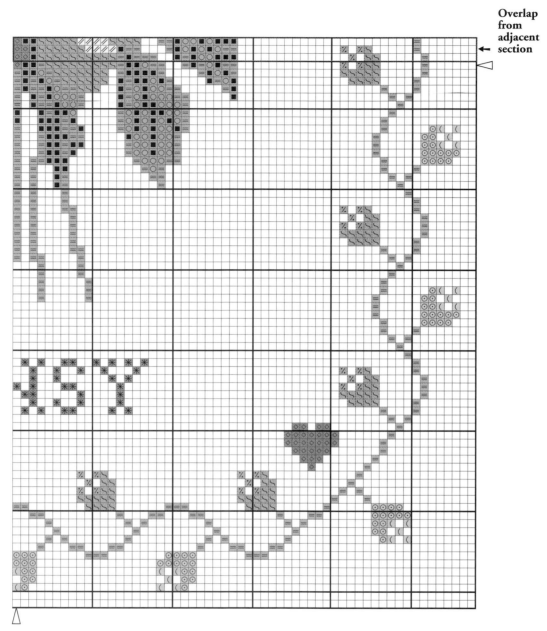

Pansy Sampler (lower right section)

Clock
♥
Chart on page 173

Materials
Stitched on 11-count Cream Aida (Zweigart #1007, #264). The fabric was cut 10" x 10". Clock face window is 7¾" x 7¾".

● Clock, 9½" x 9½" (Sudberry House #48161)

Stitch
Find and mark the center of the fabric. Line up the center of the chart with the center of the fabric. Stitching with four strands of floss, follow the cross-stitch instructions given in Cross-Stitch Basics.

Finish
Following manufacturer's instructions, mount the cross-stitched piece in the clock.

Alternate Design Sizes	
Stitches Per Inch	Design Sizes
11	7¾" x 7¾"
14	6" x 6"
18	4¾" x 4¾"
22	3¾" x 3¾"

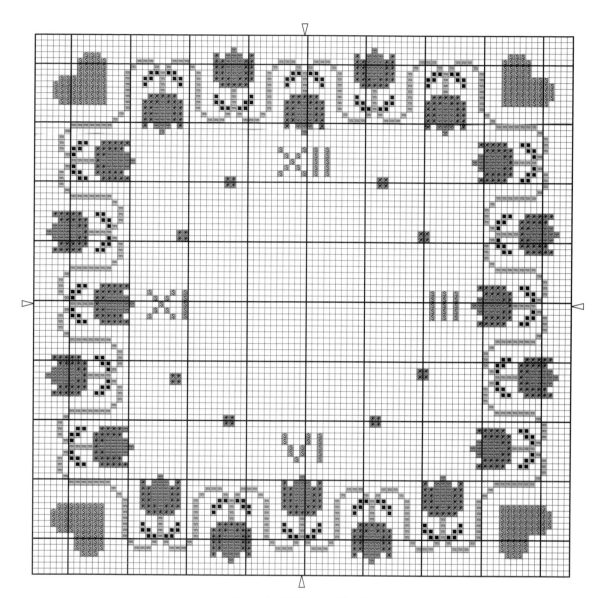

Botanical Flowers Clock

CLOCK AND TEA TRAY KEY

Note: *For each, use 1 skein of all floss colors. Cross-stitch using 2 strands floss.*

ANCHOR		DMC	COLOR
109	∽	209	Dk. Lavender
100	✳	327	Vy. Dk. Violet
24	✕	776	Med. Pink
59	∴	326	Vy. Deep Rose
160	(	827	Vy. Lt. Blue
978	⊙	322	Vy. Lt. Navy Blue

ANCHOR		DMC	COLOR
877	⊡	502	Blue Green
878	◆	501	Dk. Blue Green
215	=	320	Med. Pistachio
218	■	319	Vy. Dk. Pistachio
119	Ŝ	333	Vy. Dk. Blue Violet
307	△	783	Med. Topaz
11	+	350	Med. Coral
9	8	352	Lt. Coral
52	╱	899	Med. Rose
43	●	815	Med. Garnet

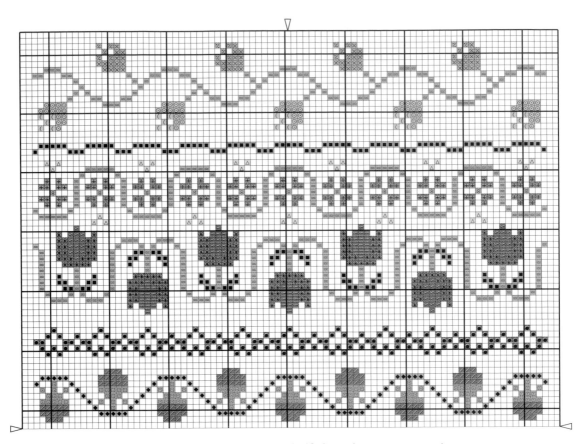

Botanical Flowers Tea Tray (half chart, key on page 173)

Tea Tray

♥

Chart shown above

Materials

Stitched on 14-count Cream Aida (Zweigart #3706, #264). The fabric was cut 7¾" x 11¾". Finished tray opening is 5¾" x 9¾".

● Tea tray, 8" x 12" (Sudberry House #80031)

Stitch

Find and mark the center of the fabric. Center and line up the upper edge of the half chart with the center of the fabric.

Follow the cross-stitch instructions given in Cross-Stitch Basics. Then stitch design in reverse from the center out, repeating the first row.

Finish

Following manufacturer's instructions, mount the cross-stitched piece in the tea tray.

Alternate Design Sizes	
Stitches Per Inch	Design Sizes
11	7¾" x 12"
14	6¼" x 9¼"
18	4½" x 7½"
22	4" x 5"

Pillow

♥

Materials

Stitched on 18-count Cream Aida (Zweigart #3793, #264). The fabric was cut 9½" x 9½". Finished pillow size is 7½" in diameter.

- White fabric for pillow back: 8½" x 8½"
- Dark Green twisted rope braid piping, ¼" diameter: 24"
- Polyester stuffing
- Potpourri (optional)
- Fray Check™
- Sewing thread to match fabric

Stitch

Find and mark the center of the fabric. Use the pansy motif from the sampler chart, omitting border and lettering. Line up the center of the motif with the center of the fabric. Stitching with one strand of floss, follow the cross-stitch instructions given in Cross-Stitch Basics.

Finish

Keeping the design centered, trim the cross-stitched piece to a circle 8½ inches in diameter. Also, cut a matching circle from the pillow back fabric. Pin trim in place on front of pillow, with braid facing in, ½ inch from edges. Cross ends over one another. Stitch in place. With right sides together, pin and stitch the circles together, taking a ½-inch seam and leaving a small opening for turning and stuffing. Grade and notch seam allowances, turn right side out, and stuff, adding potpourri if desired. Slipstitch the opening closed.

Alternate Design Sizes	
Stitches Per Inch	Design Sizes
11	4¾" x 7"
14	3¾" x 5½"
18	3" x 4¼"
22	2½" x 3½"

Note Cards

♥

Materials

Stitched on 14-count Cream Aida (Zweigart #3706, #264). The fabric was cut 5" x 7". Finished note card size is 5" x 7".

- Note cards, 5" x 7", with matching envelopes
- Craft glue
- Craft knife
- Ruler
- White paper

Stitch

Find and mark the center of the fabric. Line up the center of the flower name from the sampler chart with the center of the fabric. Follow the cross-stitch instructions given in Cross-Stitch Basics. Cross-stitch a single-row border around the flower name, two threads from the lettering.

Finish

Measure and mark the position of the cross-stitched design on the front of the note card. Using the craft knife and ruler, neatly cut an opening ⅛ inch larger all around than the lettering area. With right side up, position the cross-stitched design on the wrong side

of the note card so the design is centered in the opening. Glue in place, keeping glue away from edges of card and opening. Trim the fabric to ⅛ inch smaller all around than the card. Cut a piece of white paper the same size for backing. Glue the backing paper to the wrong side of the cross-stitched piece. Allow card to dry completely, weighted down on a flat surface.

Alternate Design Sizes	
Stitches Per Inch	Design Sizes
11	¾" x 1¾" to 5½"
14	½" x 1½" to 4¼"
18	⅜" x 1" to 3½"
22	¼" x ⅞" to 2¾"

Folk Art Flowers

The hooked rugs of
the early 19th century were
the inspiration for this fabulous
Folk Art Pillow. Stitched
with wool, the colors resemble
the natural-dyed yarns and
fabrics that were used at that
time. Thanks to strong colors and
the charming simplicity of the
flowers, the overall effect
of this group of designs is rich
and elegant.

♥

Enlarged, the geometric floral
border motif makes a
perfect design for a cozy Lap
Robe. Other variations of
the border are repeated on the
Picture Frame Mat and
Photo Album cover, along with
an urn of flowers adapted
from the pillow design.

Folk Art Pillow

♥

Chart on pages 182-83

Materials

Stitched over two threads on 20-count Christmas Green Valerie (Zweigart #3256, #685). The pillow requires ½ yard of fabric. Finished pillow size is 18" x 9½".

- Green fabric for lining: ½ yard
- Cable cord, ½" diameter: 1¾ yards
- Polyester stuffing
- Sewing thread to match fabric

Stitch

Cut two rectangles of the Valerie fabric, each 20 x 11 inches. Set aside remaining Valerie for welting. Find and mark the center of one rectangle. Line up the center of the chart with the center of the marked fabric. Work cross-stitch over two threads, using 2 strands of wool in needle; follow the cross-stitch instructions given in Cross-Stitch Basics.

Finish

Cut two pieces of lining fabric to the same dimensions as the Valerie fabric. Baste the lining fabric to the wrong side of each Valerie piece. For welting, cut and piece a bias strip 2 inches wide and 1¾ yards long from the reserved Valerie. Enclose the cord in the bias strip and stitch, using a zipper/cording foot. Trim the seam allowances to ½ inch. Beginning at the center bottom of the cross-stitched pillow top, with raw edges aligned and welting facing toward the center, baste the welting in place all around, easing to fit around the corners. Where ends of welting meet, remove stitching from fabric covering to expose ends of cord; trim cord so ends just meet. At one end, trim the fabric even with the cord; at the other, trim the fabric 1 inch longer than the cord. Turn this end under ½ inch and lap it over the other end; baste in place. With right sides together, pin pillow top and back together. Stitch around 3 sides and 4 corners, taking a ½-inch seam, and leaving an opening for turning and stuffing. Grade seam allowances, trim and clip corners, turn right side out and stuff. Slipstitch the opening closed.

Alternate Design Sizes	
Stitches Per Inch	Design Sizes
10	17" x 8¼"
11	15½" x 7½"
14	12¼" x 6"
18	9½" x 4½"
20	8½" x 4¼"
22	7¾" x 3¾"

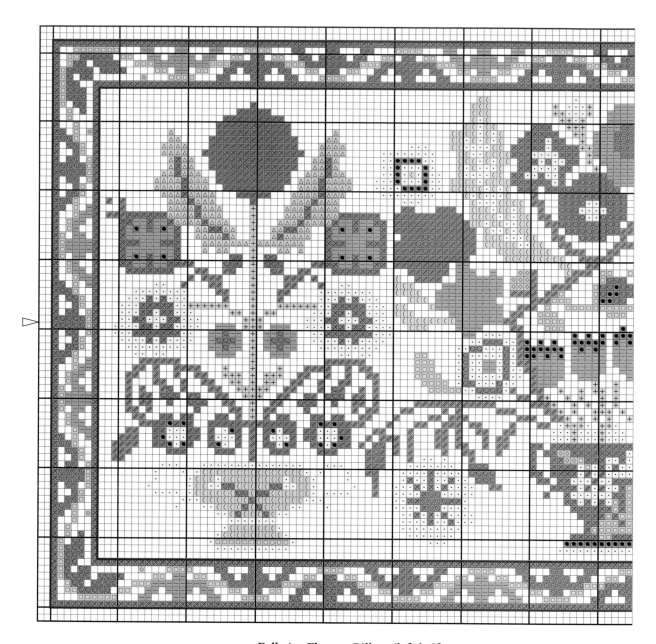

Folk Art Flowers Pillow (left half)

FOLK ART FLOWERS KEY

Note: *Thread used is DMC Broder Medicis Wool. For Pillow, use 1 skein of all colors except #8908, which requires 2. For Lap Robe, use 3 skeins of all colors except #8369, which requires 6. For Album Cover and Picture Frame, use 1 skein of each color. The number of strands of wool used is given in the directions for each project.*

Note: *#8413 is used only on the Lap Robe, #8401 and #8210 are used only on the Pillow.*

	DMC Medici	**COLOR**
╱	8139	Med. Shell Pink
◯	8129	Salmon
✕	8908	Orange Spice
●	8103	Dk. Garnet
□	8369	Seafoam Green
+	8419	Lt. Yellow Green
(	8401	Lt. Avocado Green
△	8418	Dk. Yellow Green
◆	8413	Med. Pistachio

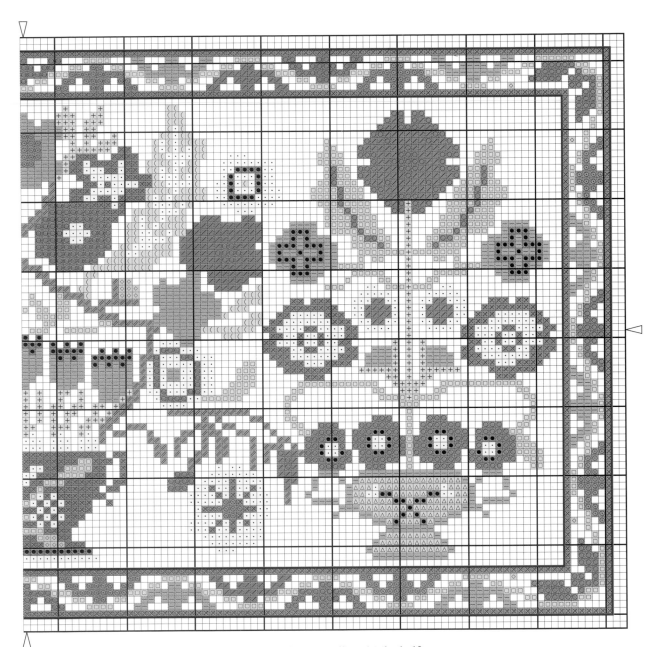

Folk Art Flowers Pillow (right half)

	DMC Medici	COLOR
•	8027	Med. Yellow
—	8484	Mustard
⊙	8302	Old Gold
⧸	8400	Khaki
◇	8210	Lt. Antique Blue

BACKSTITCH (Use 1 strand)

⌐	8103	Dk. Garnet

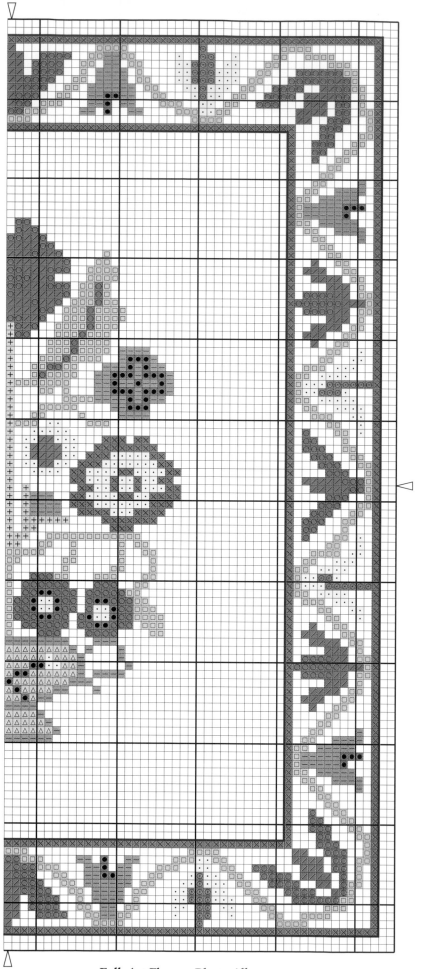

Folk Art Flowers Photo Album

Photo Album

♥

Chart on page 184

Materials

Stitched over two threads on 20-count Christmas Green Valerie (Zweigart #3256, #685). The album requires ½ yard of fabric. Finished album size is 11" x 12".

● Green felt: ½ yard
● 3-Ring photo album, 11" x 12"
● Dark Green marbled paper

See Covering A Photo Album on page 213 for additional materials.

continued

Stitch

Place the opened album on the wrong side of the Valerie fabric. Trace around the entire album cover, then trace again 1¾ inches outside original line. Also mark the hinge edge of the front cover. Find and mark the center of the front cover on the fabric. Baste a marking line through the vertical and horizontal center. Center the half chart along the vertical center line. Work cross-stitch over two threads, using two strands of wool; follow the cross-stitch instructions given in Cross-Stitch Basics. Omitting the center vertical row of stitches, stitch the center design and border design in reverse to complete.

Finish

Cut fabric along outer traced line. Then follow the instructions given on page 213 to cover the photo album. Check to see that the design stays centered on the album front as you work. Use the green felt for the padding. Use the marbled paper to cover the inside covers.

Alternate Design Sizes	
Stitches Per Inch	Design Sizes
10	9½" x 11¼"
11	8½" x 10¼"
14	6¾" x 8"
18	5¼" x 6¼"
20	4¾" x 5¾"
22	4¼" x 5"

Picture Frame Mat
♥
Chart on page 187

Materials

Stitched over two threads on 20-count Christmas Green Valerie (Zweigart #3256, #685). The fabric was cut 11" x 13". Finished mat size is 8" x 10".

- Mat board, 8" x 10" with a 4" x 6" opening for picture
- Fray Check™
- Craft glue

Stitch

At the upper left corner of the fabric, measure and mark a point 2 inches from the side and top edges. Begin stitching the outer corner of the quarter-border chart at this point. Work cross-stitch over two threads, using two strands of wool; follow the cross-stitch instructions given in Cross-Stitch Basics. Omitting the vertical row of center stitches at the top and bottom, and repeating the horizontal row of center stitches at the sides, work the quarter-border chart in reverse in each direction to stitch the next two corners, then stitch again to complete the border.

Finish

Keeping the design centered, position the embroidered piece over the mat board. Pull the excess fabric to the back and glue in place. Mark and cut out a rectangle 1 inch inside the mat board opening. Clip diagonally into each corner to aid in turning. Tape or glue fabric securely to the back of mat board. Dab inside corners with Fray Check™ to prevent fraying. Allow to dry thoroughly. Using the cardboard and backing fabric, follow the instructions on page 215 to make the frame backing.

Alternate Design Sizes	
Stitches Per Inch	Design Sizes
10	7½" x 9½"
11	7 x 8¾"
14	5½" x 7"
18	4¼" x 5½"
20	3¾" x 4¾"
22	3½" x 4½"

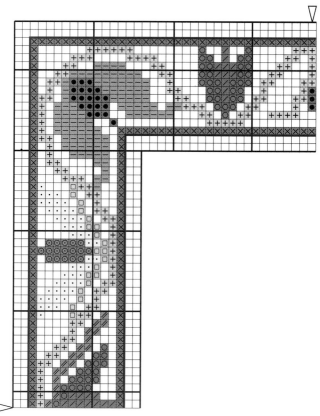

Folk Art Flowers Picture Frame Mat

FOLK ART FLOWERS KEY

Note: *Thread used is DMC Broder Medicis Wool. For Pillow, use 1 skein of all colors except #8908, which requires 2. For Lap Robe, use 3 skeins of all colors except #8369, which requires 6. For Album Cover and Picture Frame, use 1 skein of each color. The number of strands of wool used is given in the directions for each project.*

Note: *#8413 is used only on the Lap Robe, #8401 and #8210 are used only on the Pillow.*

DMC Medici	COLOR
8139	Med. Shell Pink
8129	Salmon
8908	Orange Spice

DMC Medici	COLOR
8103	Dk. Garnet
8369	Seafoam Green
8419	Lt. Yellow Green
8401	Lt. Avocado Green
8418	Dk. Yellow Green
8413	Med. Pistachio
8027	Med. Yellow
8484	Mustard
8302	Old Gold
8400	Khaki
8210	Lt. Antique Blue

BACKSTITCH (Use 1 strand)

8103	Dk. Garnet

Lap Robe

♥

Charts shown below and on page 189

Materials

Stitched over two threads on 14-count Cream Gloria Afghan (Zweigart #7517, #21). The fabric was cut 46" x 53". Finished robe size is 36" x 43".

Stitch

Find and mark the center of each woven corner block and border panel on the fabric. Work cross-stitch over two threads, using three strands of wool; follow the cross-stitch instructions given in Cross-Stitch Basics. Aligning the center of the chart and block, position the base of the flower on the corner chart toward the outer corner of each corner block. Follow the appropriate half-border charts to stitch each side border. To complete the side borders, work each chart in reverse, repeating the center row of stitches for the short sides and omitting the center row of stitches for the long sides.

Finish

Mark 5 inches in from edges all around. Unravel the threads to the marked lines to make a fringe. Knot together groups of five threads to secure into fringe.

Corner Motif Alternate Design Sizes	
Stitches Per Inch	Design Sizes
7	3¾" x 3¾"
11	2¾" x 2¾"
14	2" x 2"
18	1½" x 1½"
22	1¼" x 1¼"

Short Side Motif Alternate Design Sizes	
Stitches Per Inch	Design Sizes
7	21" x 3¾"
11	13¼" x 2¾"
14	10½" x 2"
18	8¼" x 1½"
22	6¾" x 1¼"

Long Side Motif Alternate Design Sizes	
Stitches Per Inch	Design Sizes
7	29¼" x 3¾"
11	18½" x 2¾"
14	14½" x 2"
18	11½" x 1½"
22	9¼" x 1¼"

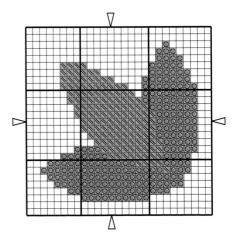

Folk Art Flowers Lap Robe (corner)

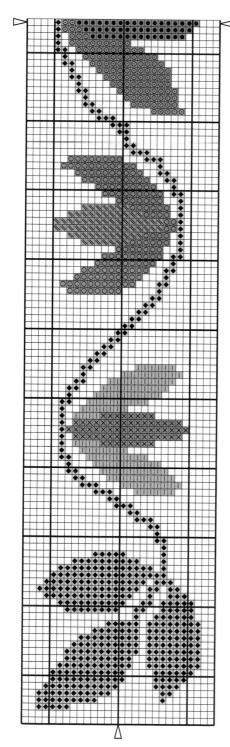

Folk Art Flowers Lap Robe (long side)

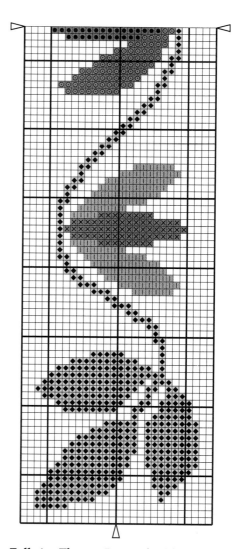

Folk Art Flowers Lap Robe (short side)

Note: *#8413 is used only on the Lap Robe, #8401 and #8210 are used only on the Pillow.*

	DMC Medici	COLOR
╱	8139	Med. Shell Pink
⊙	8129	Salmon
✕	8908	Orange Spice
●	8103	Dk. Garnet
☐	8369	Seafoam Green
+	8419	Lt. Yellow Green
(	8401	Lt. Avocado Green
△	8418	Dk. Yellow Green
◆	8413	Med. Pistachio
·	8027	Med. Yellow
I	8484	Mustard
⊙	8302	Old Gold
◥	8400	Khaki
◇	8210	Lt. Antique Blue

BACKSTITCH (Use 1 strand)		
⌐	8103	Dk. Garnet

FOLK ART FLOWERS KEY

Note: *Thread used is DMC Broder Medicis Wool. For Pillow, use 1 skein of all colors except #8908, which requires 2. For Lap Robe, use 3 skeins of all colors except #8369, which requires 6. For Album Cover and Picture Frame, use 1 skein of each color. The number of strands of wool used is given in the directions for each project.*

Christmas Flowers

Christmas is
truly a time of love and sharing.
The flowers of Christmas
add color to the winter holidays
and symbolize the new
life that the season represents.

♥

Evergreen swags, poinsettias
and Christmas roses adorn this
lush Holiday Sampler, made
even more festive with glittering
metallic threads. Many of the
design elements on the sampler
can easily be used to create
small projects such as the
Christmas Rose, Wreath and
Swag, and Angel ornaments,
as well as the Poinsettia
Stocking and the Christmas
Cards, all shown here.

Holiday Sampler

Chart on pages 194-97

Materials

Stitched on 14-count Gold Metallic/Cream Aida (Zweigart #3706, #118). The fabric was cut 15½" x 20". Finished size of framed sampler as shown is 13½" x 18".

Stitch

Find and mark the center of the fabric. Line up the center of the chart with the center of the fabric. Follow the cross-stitch instructions given in Cross-Stitch Basics.

Finish

For best results, have this piece professionally matted and framed.

Alternate Design Sizes	
Stitches Per Inch	Design Sizes
11	13½" x 18"
14	10½" x 14"
18	8¼" x 11"
22	6¾" x 9"

Christmas Flowers Holiday Sampler (upper left section)

CHRISTMAS FLOWERS KEY

Note: *Use 1 skein of all floss colors except DMC #702, #349, #704, and #3706, which require 2. Cross-stitch using 2 strands floss.*

ANCHOR		DMC	COLOR
	•		1019 Pink Marlitt
881	/	945	Med. Sportsman Beige
893	○	224	Vy. Lt. Shell Pink
33	□	3706	Med. Melon
35	+	3705	Dk. Melon
13	✕	349	Dk. Coral
1006	●	304	Med. Christmas Red
897	■	902	Vy. Dk. Garnet
1043	·	369	Vy. Lt. Pistachio

ANCHOR		DMC	COLOR
238	/	703	Chartreuse
255	○	907	Lt. Parrot Green
256	□	704	Bright Chartreuse
214	+	368	Lt. Pistachio Green
226	✕	702	Kelly Green
258	●	904	Vy. Dk. Forest Green
212	■	561	Vy. Dk. Jade
108	/	210	Med. Lavender
110	/	208	Vy. Dk. Lavender
102	■	550	Vy. Dk. Violet
275	·	746	Off White
31	/	3708	Lt. Melon
295	●	726	Lt. Topaz
	+	280	Gold Metallic
303	✕	742	Lt. Tangerine

Christmas Flowers Holiday Sampler (upper right section)

ANCHOR		DMC	COLOR
	·		1059 Lt. Blue Marlitt
136	□	799	Med Delft
281	+	732	Olive Green
1049	×	301	Med. Mahogany
380	■	838	Vy. Dk. Beige Brown
	□	281	Silver Metallic
		BACKSTITCH	
246	⌐	986	Vy. Dk. Forest Green, 2 strands
	⌐	280	Gold Metallic, 2 strands
	⌐	281	Silver Metallic, 2 strands
281	⌐	732	Olive Green, 1 strand
382	⌐	3371	Black Brown, 1 strand

ANCHOR		DMC	COLOR
		FRENCH KNOTS (strands/wrap)	
13	●	349	Dk. Coral (2/1)
380	●	838	Vy. Dk. Beige Brown (2/1)
303	●	742	Lt. Tangerine (2/2)
303	●	742	Lt. Tangerine (3/2)
1001	●	976	Med. Golden Brown (2/2)
295	○	726	Lt. Topaz (2/2)
	●	281	Silver Metallic

Overlap from adjacent section ↗

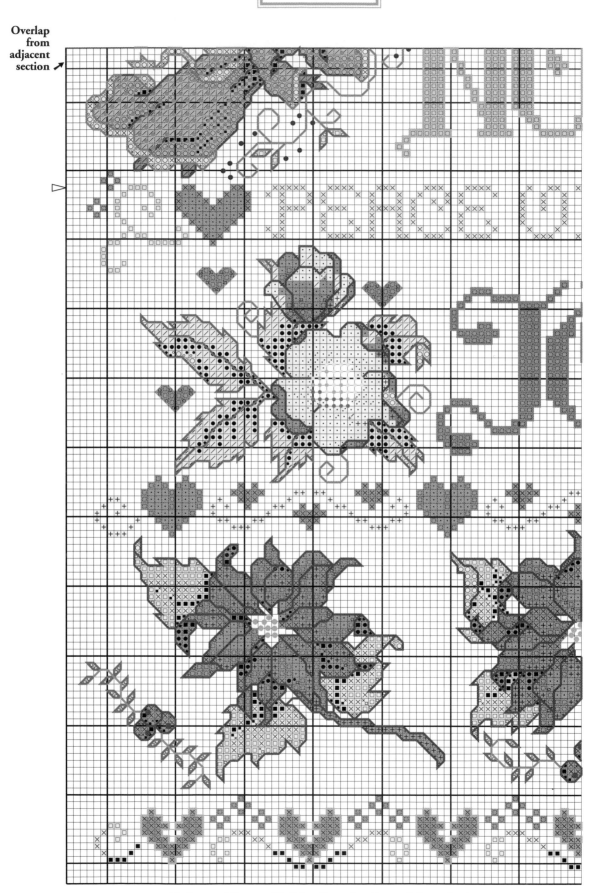

Christmas Flowers Holiday Sampler (lower left section)

Overlap
from
adjacent
section

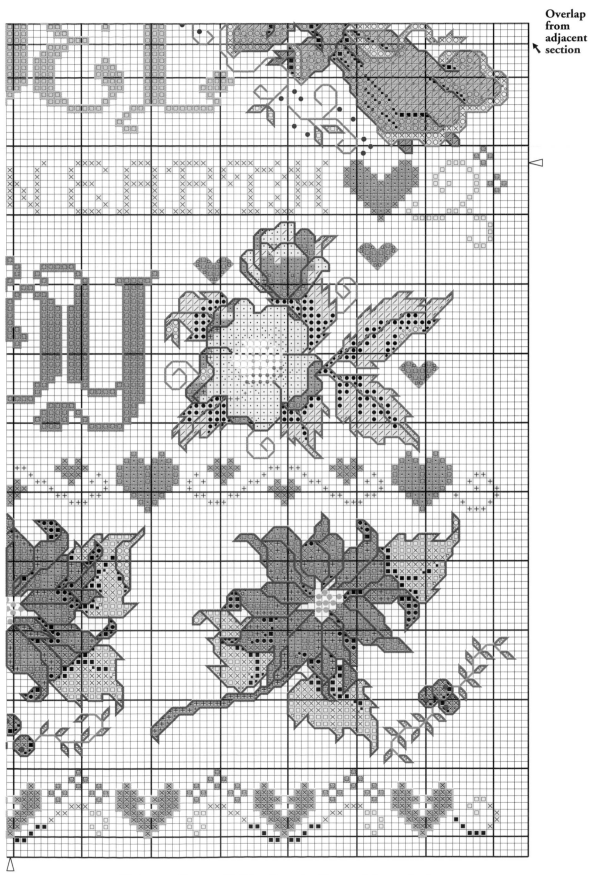

Christmas Flowers Holiday Sampler (lower right section)

Angel Ornament

♥

Materials

Stitched on 14-count Antique White Aida (Zweigart #3706, #101). The fabric was cut 6" x 12" (includes ornament back). Finished ornament size is 4¼" x 4¼", excluding lace.

● Pregathered gold-edged lace trim, 1" wide: 19"

- Fine gold braid: 6"
- Polyester stuffing
- Sewing thread to match fabric

Stitch

From the fabric, cut one 6 x 6 inch square. Find and mark the center of the fabric square. Using the angel motif from the sampler chart, line up the center of the motif with the center of the fabric square. Follow the cross-stitch instructions given in Cross-Stitch Basics.

Finish

Keeping the design centered, trim the cross-stitched piece to a 5¼ x 5¼ inch square. Cut a matching square from the remaining fabric. With right sides together, pin and baste the gathered lace around the cross-stitched ornament front, with the gold edge facing toward the center. Sew the short ends of the lace together, finishing the seam neatly. With right sides together, stitch the front and back pieces together, taking a ½-inch seam, and leaving a 3-inch opening along one side for turning. Grade seam allowances and trim corners. Turn right side out, stuff, and slipstitch the opening closed. Tie the ends of braid into a knot to make a loop for hanging. Tack the knot to the center of the top edge, behind the lace.

Alternate Design Sizes	
Stitches Per Inch	Design Sizes
11	4½" x 3¾"
14	3½" x 3"
18	2¾" x 2¼"
22	2¼" x 2"

Christmas Rose Ornament

♥

Materials

Stitched on 14-count Victorian Christmas Red Aida (Zweigart # 3706, #969). The fabric was cut 7" x 11". Finished ornament size is approximately 5" x 4½".

- Red rope-twist braid, ¼" in diameter: 18"
- Red satin ribbon, ⅛" wide: 12"
- Polyester stuffing
- Transfer paper
- Fray Check™
- Sewing thread to match fabric

Stitch

Using the transfer paper and adding ½-inch seam allowance all around pattern, draw two hearts on the Aida cloth (page 200). Do not cut out yet. Find and mark the center of one heart. Using the Christmas rose motif from the sampler chart, line up the center of the motif with the center of the fabric. Follow the cross-stitch instructions given in Cross-Stitch Basics to work the design on one heart.

Finish

Cut out the hearts. With right sides together, pin hearts together and stitch, taking a ½-inch seam and leaving a 3-inch opening along one side for turning. Grade seam allowances, clip/notch curves, and turn right side out. Stuff, then slipstitch the opening

continued

closed. Beginning and ending at center top, sew the braid around the edges of the ornament. Dab ends of the braid with Fray Check™ to prevent fraying. Cut ribbon in half, tie into a small bow, and tack to top of heart. Tie the ends of remaining ribbon into a knot to make a loop for hanging. Tack knot at top back of heart.

Alternate Design Sizes	
Stitches Per Inch	Design Sizes
11	3¾" x 3"
14	3" x 2½"
18	2¼" x 2"
22	2" x 1½"

Christmas Rose Ornament

Wreath and Swag Ornament

♥

Materials

Stitched on 14-count Antique White Aida (Zweigart #3706, #101). The fabric was cut 6" x 18". Finished ornament size is a cylinder 5" high x 3¼" in diameter.

continued

- Christmas print fabric: 6" x 11"
- Lightweight cardboard: 3" x 10"
- Red embroidery floss for tassel: 1 skein
- Gold thread
- Red rope-twist braid, ¼" diameter: 20"
- Red satin ribbon, ⅛" wide: 6"
- Polyester stuffing
- Fray Check™
- Sewing thread to match fabric

Stitch

Find and mark the center of the fabric. Using the wreath and swag motif from the sampler chart, line up the center of the motif with the center of the fabric. Follow the cross-stitch instructions given in Cross-Stitch Basics.

Finish

Keeping the design centered, trim the cross-stitched piece to a rectangle 3 inches high and 11 inches long. Cut the print fabric into two pieces, each 3 x 11 inches. With right sides together, stitch one print piece to each long edge of the cross-stitched piece, taking

½-inch seams. Turn each remaining long edge of print fabric under ½ inch; press. Machine-stitch or hand-sew gathering stitches along the pressed edges, leaving long thread ends. With right sides together, fold piece crosswise and stitch shorter edges together to form a cylinder with the cross-stitched section in the center and the print sections at top and bottom (see Diagram, below). Pull up the gathering threads at the bottom of the ornament tightly enough to close; knot to secure. Turn right side out. Flex the cardboard crosswise into a cylinder, rolling it over the edge of a table or counter to cause it to curl. Butt the short ends and tape them together. Insert in the ornament, behind the cross-stitched section, lining up the taped seam with the stitched seam. Stuff. Gather the top edge and secure.

Cut two pieces of braid, each 10 inches long. Glue or sew one piece over each circumference seam. Dab ends of the braid with Fray Check™ to prevent fraying. Using red embroidery floss, make a tassel 3½ inches long. Wrap the gold thread 9 times around the tassel, 1 inch down from the top. Knot to secure. Trim ends even. Tack the tassel in the center of the gathers at bottom of ornament. Tie the ends of the ribbon into a knot to make a loop for hanging. Tack the knot at center top of ornament.

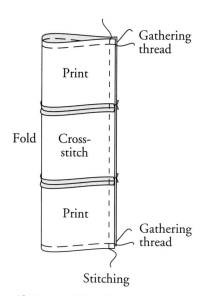

Christmas Wreath Ornament

Alternate Design Sizes	
Stitches Per Inch	Design Sizes
11	12" x 3"
14	9½" x 2½"
18	7½" x 2"
22	6" x 1½"

Poinsettia Stocking

♥

Chart on page 204

Materials
Stitched over two threads on Green Velvet
Stocking with 28-count linen cuff (Charles
Craft #SG-4026-3600). The stocking is
14" long x 11" wide; the front of the cuff
is 7" x 4 ½".

continued

Stitch

Find and mark the center of the cuff front. Line up the center of the chart with the center of the cuff front. Follow the cross-stitch instructions given in Cross-Stitch Basics.

Finish

The stocking requires no finishing.

Alternate Design Sizes	
Stitches Per Inch	Design Sizes
11	5¾" x 4¾"
14	4½" x 3¾"
18	3½" x 3"
22	2¾" x 2½"

Christmas Cards

♥

Charts on pages 206, 207

Materials

Stitched on 14-count Antique White Aida (Zweigart #3706, #101). The fabric was cut 5" x 7". Finished card is 5" x 7".

- Note cards, 5" x 7"
- Craft glue
- Craft knife
- Ruler and oval template
- White paper

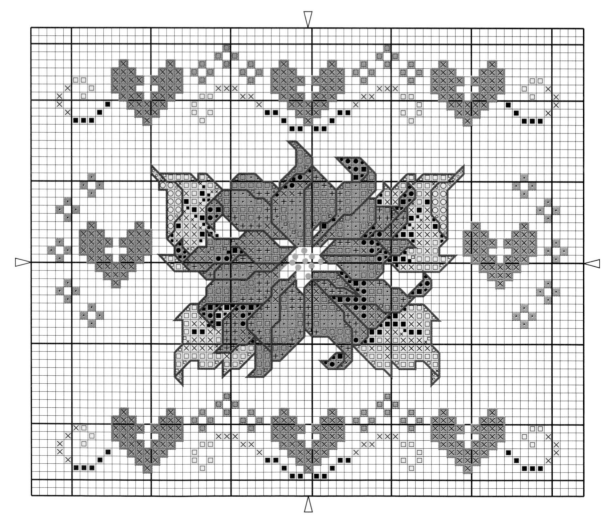

Christmas Flowers Poinsettia Stocking

Stitch

Find and mark the center of the fabric. Line up the center of the chart with the center of the fabric. Follow the cross-stitch instructions given in Cross-Stitch Basics.

Finish

Measure and mark the position of the cross-stitched design on the front of the note card. Using the craft knife and ruler, neatly cut an opening ⅛ inch larger all around than the design area. With right side up, position the cross-stitched design on the wrong side of the note card so the design is centered in the opening. Glue in place, keeping glue away from edges of card and opening. Trim the fabric to ⅛ inch smaller all around than the card. Cut a piece of white paper the same size for backing. Glue the backing paper to the wrong side of the cross-stitched piece. Allow card to dry completely, weighted down on a flat surface.

Alternate Design Sizes	
Stitches Per Inch	Design Sizes
11	6" x 3¾"
14	4¾" x 3"
18	3¾" x 2¼"
22	3" x 1¾"

CHRISTMAS FLOWERS KEY

Note: *Use 1 skein of all floss colors except DMC #702, #349, #704, and #3706, which require 2. Cross-stitch using 2 strands floss.*

ANCHOR		DMC	COLOR
	·		1019 Pink Marlitt
881	/	945	Med. Sportsman Beige
893	O	224	Vy. Lt. Shell Pink
33	□	3706	Med. Melon
35	+	3705	Dk. Melon
13	X	349	Dk. Coral
1006	●	304	Med. Christmas Red
897	■	902	Vy. Dk. Garnet
1043	·	369	Vy. Lt. Pistachio
238	/	703	Chartreuse
255	O	907	Lt. Parrot Green
256	□	704	Bright Chartreuse
214	+	368	Lt. Pistachio Green
226	X	702	Kelly Green
258	●	904	Vy. Dk. Forest Green
212	■	561	Vy. Dk. Jade
108	/	210	Med. Lavender
110	O	208	Vy. Dk. Lavender
102	■	550	Vy. Dk. Violet
275	·	746	Off White
31	/	3708	Lt. Melon

ANCHOR		DMC	COLOR
295	O	726	Lt. Topaz
	+	280	Gold Metallic
303	X	742	Lt. Tangerine
	·		1059 Lt. Blue Marlitt
136	□	799	Med. Delft
281	+	732	Olive Green
1049	X	301	Med. Mahogany
380	■	838	Vy. Dk. Beige Brown
	□	281	Silver Metallic
BACKSTITCH			
246	⌐	986	Vy. Dk. Forest Green, 2 strands
	⌐	280	Gold Metallic, 2 strands
	⌐	281	Silver Metallic, 2 strands
281	⌐	732	Olive Green, 1 strand
382	⌐	3371	Black Brown, 1 strand
FRENCH KNOTS (strands/wrap)			
13	●	349	Dk. Coral (2/1)
380	●	838	Vy. Dk. Beige Brown (2/1)
303	●	742	Lt. Tangerine (2/2)
303	●	742	Lt. Tangerine (3/2)
1001	●	976	Med. Golden Brown (2/2)
295	○	726	Lt. Topaz (2/2)
	●	281	Silver Metallic

Joy Christmas Card

CHRISTMAS FLOWERS KEY

Note: *Use* 1 skein of all floss colors that are indicated on the chart for the card that you select. Cross-stitch using 2 strands of floss.

ANCHOR		DMC	COLOR
	·		1019 Pink Marlitt
881	/	945	Med. Sportsman Beige
893	○	224	Vy. Lt. Shell Pink
33	□	3706	Med. Melon
35	+	3705	Dk. Melon
13	×	349	Dk. Coral
1006	●	304	Med. Christmas Red
897	■	902	Vy. Dk. Garnet
1043	·	369	Vy. Lt. Pistachio

ANCHOR		DMC	COLOR
238	/	703	Chartreuse
255	○	907	Lt. Parrot Green
256	□	704	Bright Chartreuse
214	+	368	Lt. Pistachio Green
226	×	702	Kelly Green
258	●	904	Vy. Dk. Forest Green
212	■	561	Vy. Dk. Jade
108	/	210	Med. Lavender
110	○	208	Vy. Dk. Lavender
102	■	550	Vy. Dk. Violet
275	·	746	Off White
31	/	3708	Lt. Melon
295	●	726	Lt. Topaz
	+	280	Gold Metallic
303	×	742	Lt. Tangerine

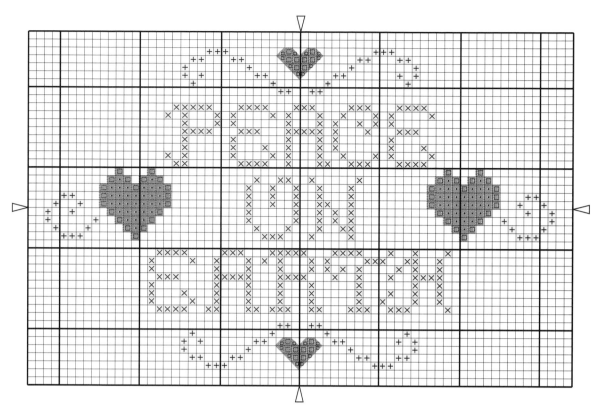

Peace on Earth Christmas Card

ANCHOR		DMC	COLOR
	·		1059 Lt. Blue Marlitt
136	□	799	Med Delft
281	+	732	Olive Green
1049	×	301	Med. Mahogany
380	■	838	Vy. Dk. Beige Brown
	□	281	Silver Metallic
		BACKSTITCH	
246		986	Vy. Dk. Forest Green, 2 strands
		280	Gold Metallic, 2 strands
		281	Silver Metallic, 2 strands
281		732	Olive Green, 1 strand
382		3371	Black Brown, 1 strand

ANCHOR		DMC	COLOR
		FRENCH KNOTS (strands/wrap)	
13	●	349	Dk. Coral (2/1)
380	●	838	Vy. Dk. Beige Brown (2/1)
303	●	742	Lt. Tangerine (2/2)
303	●	742	Lt. Tangerine (3/2)
1001	●	976	Med. Golden Brown (2/2)
295	○	726	Lt. Topaz (2/2)
	●	281	Silver Metallic

Cross-Stitch Basics

Getting Started

Cross-stitching consists mainly of X-shaped stitches formed by running threads through the holes in an even-weave fabric. This fabric has threads evenly spaced vertically and horizontally to form a gridlike pattern and is available in many types and colors. The "count," or holes per inch, given for the fabric indicates how many stitches can be made per inch. Thus, stitching on a fabric with a count that is different from what is called for in the directions will result in a smaller or larger stitching area.

On the project charts, each symbol represents one cross-stitch, and a different symbol is used for each color of floss (see Figures 1-3). Backstitches are represented by straight lines, with the floss color given on the color key for each chart. A key to the symbols, showing the color names and floss numbers for both Anchor and DMC floss, is provided for each project.

The horizontal and vertical centers of the designs are marked with arrows on the chart. Find the center of your fabric by folding it in half in either direction and creasing the folds; unfold the fabric, and use straight pins or running stitches to mark these center folds. Stitch the design in the center of the fabric first, comparing the position of the stitches on the graph to the position on the fabric, and work out from there.

Generally the number of strands of floss used for cross-stitching is:
> 3 strands for 11 count
> 2 strands for 14 count and
> 1 strand for 18 count.

However, some stitchers prefer a fuller look and use one additional strand for each count.

Materials

Fabrics
In this book, you will find projects that call for different even-weave fabrics, ready-made fabric items with even-weave inserts, and plain fabrics to be stitched using waste canvas for its even-weave guidelines. You can choose from a wide selection of even-weave fabrics. Colors range over the entire spectrum, and counts vary from 7 per inch to almost 30 per inch. Fiber content varies too, from 100 percent linen or cotton to blends of natural and synthetic fibers. Some fabrics are made entirely of synthetic fibers. Select fabrics that comfortably match your stitching style and project needs.

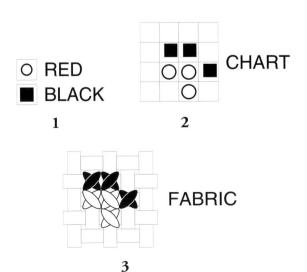

○ RED
■ BLACK

1

CHART

2

FABRIC

3

Most stitchers prefer to hold their fabric taut and straight in a stitchery frame or embroidery hoop. While this is optional for very small projects, it does make stitching easier in most cases.

General Materials Needed

- Embroidery scissors
- Sewing machine (for some projects)
- Embroidery hoop (optional but recommended)
- Iron

See individual project instructions for other materials.

Floss and Special Threads

Floss is composed of six strands of thread. For cross-stitching, cut an 18-inch length; separate out the desired number of strands for stitching with one hand, hold the rest in the other hand, and pull the strands apart, letting the floss twist away at the other end as you pull. Refer to the Color Key for each project to determine the number of strands to use.

Metallic thread may be used by itself, but it has more impact when used with floss in a matching color. Thus, if metallic gold is specified in the color key, use one strand of metallic gold and one strand of plain gold floss. If you prefer to omit metallic floss when it is called for, you may substitute a similar color of plain floss.

Quantities of floss needed vary from project to project. Generally, one skein of a color is enough for a project in this book. If more than one skein is needed, the instructions will specify how many are needed.

Needles

Tapestry needles, size 24 or 26, are used for most cross-stitching on even-weave fabrics or perforated paper. They have blunt points that slip through the holes in the fabric or paper easily. Embroidery needles—with sharp points—are best for cross-stitching using waste canvas on regular fabrics. If you are cross-stitching with glass beads, use a thin quilting needle (size 11).

Embellishments

Charms, lace, braid, ribbons, and buttons can be sewn or glued onto cross-stitched projects with washable fabric or craft glue.

Stitching Hints

Begin a project by cross-stitching the center of the charted design in the center of the fabric. The most successful method of cross-stitching is to pass your needle entirely down through the fabric before bringing it back up to the front again. This allows you to keep the floss even and does not distort the fabric. Unless otherwise indicated, do not knot the floss; hold a ½-inch tail of floss on the back of the fabric and cross-stitch over it with your first several cross-stitches to secure it. To end a thread, run the floss under several cross-stitches on the back to secure (see Figure 4). Cut off excess.

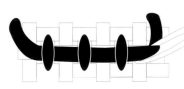

4

Cross-stitching
Over One or Two Threads

Most cross-stitching is worked over one thread or square of the fabric, passing the needle from the back up through one hole, then down through the next diagonal hole. To make stitching more prominent, some designs are cross-stitched over two threads or squares of the fabric, passing the needle up through one hole, skipping the next diagonal hole, and going back down through the second diagonal hole. Your project instructions will specify if you should work over more than one thread.

Stitches

The following instructions detail the basic stitches used to make the projects in this book.

Cross-stitch

Each individual cross-stitch is made up of two stitches that together form an X (see Figure 5). The bottom stitch is worked from lower left to upper right. The top stitch is worked from lower right to upper left. Do a row of bottom stitches first, working from left to right (see Figure 6). Complete the X's by working the top stitches from right to left (see Figure 6).

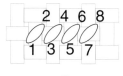

5

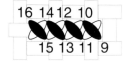

6

Partial Cross-stitch

Occasionally the squares on the chart contain one or two small symbols. These indicate one-quarter or three-quarter cross-stitches, which are used to obtain rounded shapes. Make them as shown in Figure 7.

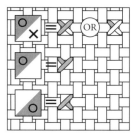

7

Backstitch

Backstitching is shown on the cross-stitch chart in heavy lines. It is used to define shapes by forming a continuous line around them or to create lettering. Backstitches can go diagonally across one or two squares of fabric or straight around the perimeter of a fabric square. Do backstitching once the cross-stitching is complete.

Figure 8 illustrates backstitching. The needle comes up at 1, goes down at 2, comes up at 3, goes down at 4 (the same hole as 1), comes up at 5, and goes down at 6 (the same hole as 3). With this method, the thread travels twice as far on the back of the fabric as on the front, and holes are used more than once.

8

French Knot

French knots are shown as dots on the charts; stitch these after all other stitching is completed: Tie a knot in the end of the floss. Bring the needle up from the back of fabric until the knot is against the fabric; pull the floss taut. Hold the needle close to the fabric (at the place it came through the fabric), and wrap the floss around the needle one, two, or three times, as indicated in your project directions (see Figure 9). Hold the floss coming off the needle firmly near the fabric, and, keeping the floss taut with one hand, reinsert the needle close to where it first came through with the other hand (see Figure 10). Pull the needle and floss through to the back of the fabric; tie a knot on the back, and trim the excess floss.

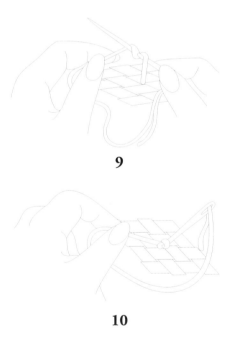

9

10

Lazy Daisy Stitch

Bring the needle up from the back of the fabric. Go back through the same hole, leaving a loop of floss on the top of the fabric. Bring the needle up through a nearby hole,

and position it inside the floss loop (see Figure 11). Pull the thread tight. Pass the needle over the floss to the outside of the loop, and take it back down through the second hole (see Figure 12). Secure the thread on the back when all stitches are complete.

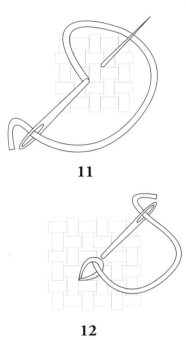

11

12

Correcting Mistakes

Everyone makes mistakes—especially in stitching. If you used the wrong color or made a mistake in counting the placement of a stitch or stitches, first decide whether it is worth correcting. Some mistakes will go unnoticed, like the center of a flower being one square too small. But some errors, such as in symmetrical designs or letters, will need to be corrected. Identify the stitches you need to remove; use tiny scissors with sharp points or specially designed thread snips to cut the threads on the back side of the fabric. When the stitches are clipped, pull the remaining threads out of the fabric with tweezers and restitch.

Techniques with Special Materials

Glass Beads

When cross-stitching beads onto fabric, stitch all of them on the same angle, using a half cross-stitch. Use only one strand of floss to attach the beads (unless your project instructions specify otherwise); for best results, match the color of the floss to the color of the beads. Use a size 11 quilting needle or other sharp, thin embroidery needle. Bring the needle up through the fabric, through a bead, and down through the next diagonal hole, completing a half cross-stitch. Each bead may seem loose until you stitch the next one on.

Keep a few beads at a time in a small container such as a plastic lid. This makes them easier to thread onto the needle. Start and finish the floss just as you do in traditional cross-stitching.

Waste Canvas

Waste canvas is a stiff grid of threads that acts as a guide when cross-stitching on fabrics that do not have an even weave. Follow our easy directions for using waste canvas.

Materials Needed for Working with Waste Canvas

- Embroidery scissors
- Tweezers
- All-purpose sewing pins
- Sewing needle and thread
- Rescue tape (optional)
- Sponge or spray bottle
- Embroidery or chenille needle

Cut waste canvas to the size specified in the project instructions (about ½ inch larger all around than the finished design size). To center the design on clothing, fold the garment in half lengthwise. Measure down this center fold to where you want the top of your design to start, and mark the location with a pin. Measure to find the center of the canvas. Line up the center of the canvas with the center fold of the garment, using the blue threads of the canvas as guidelines for placing the canvas on the straight grain of the fabric. Pin canvas in place, with top edge about ½ inch above the top of the design area. To keep the canvas securely in place, baste around all edges or use Rescue tape, a double-sided tape made especially for use on fabrics.

If desired, stretch the area to be worked in an embroidery hoop. Cross-stitch the design, using the large holes (not the small ones) where the threads of the waste canvas intersect. When working with waste canvas, knot the floss on the back when starting and ending a thread to make it more secure. After stitching, remove the basting thread or tape, and carefully trim the canvas close to the edges of the stitched design.

To remove the remaining canvas, dampen the threads with a sponge or spray bottle of water to soften the fibers. Using tweezers, pull out the horizontal and vertical threads of the canvas, one at a time.

Stitching Letters and Numbers

Some of the projects in this book use lettering in the design. In most cases, simply follow the chart. Where you will add a name and/or date, an alphabet and numbers have been provided in a separate chart, and the area to be personalized left blank on the main chart. To use these alphabets, either 1) trace the needed letters/numbers onto transparent chart paper, 2) copy the letters onto blank chart paper, or 3) photocopy the alphabet a few times, then cut and paste as needed to create the desired design.

Covering a Photo Album

Materials (see project instructions for amounts)
● Photo album: Ring-binder type
● Cross-stitched fabric piece
● Fabric for lining (firmly woven cotton or similar)
● Batting: 1 inch thick (or other padding)
● Ruler
● Felt-tip pen
● Scissors
● Thick white glue
● Lightweight poster board

Directions (see Figures 12-17)
NOTE: Check the fit of the fabric as you work to be sure the album will close when covered; adjust as necessary before glue is set, keeping design in position on front cover. Remove album pages while covering album; replace when glue is dry.

1. Place opened album on wrong side of lining fabric. Trace around the album with felt-tip pen. Add 1¾ inches all around, and cut out. See Figure 13.

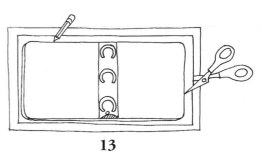

13

2. Place opened album on batting. Trace around it with felt-tip pen and cut out. See Figure 14.

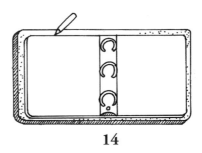

14

3. Cut two strips of lining fabric 1½ inches wide x ½ inch longer than the spine of the album. Turn ends under ¼ inch; press. Apply a thin bead of glue down groove on each side of metal ring bar in center of album. Glue down fabric strips as close to the bar as possible, or pry metal up slightly and slip fabric underneath, then glue down remaining edges of fabric. See Figure 15.

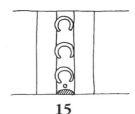

15

4. With wrong sides together, layer the embroidered piece and the fabric cut in Step 1. With lining side up, place layered fabrics on work surface; place batting in center. Place opened album on top of batting. Apply thin dab of glue to all corners on inside of album cover. See Figure 16. Pull fabric over edges of album front and press into glue at corners. Gently close album to allow fabric to stretch around spine, then pull fabric over edges of back cover and press into glue at corners.

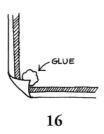

16

5. At bottom end of metal bar, cut two slits in fabric extending straight down from each edge of the spine. Turn fabric up at end of bar, trimming to fit just underneath. Apply thin layer of glue along bottom edge of inside of album. Bring edges of fabric over glue and smooth in place; work cut edges under metal bar, if possible. See Figure 17.

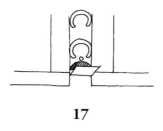

17

6. Turn the album so the top edges are at the bottom and repeat the previous step, pulling the fabric taut to eliminate wrinkles.

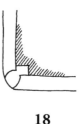

18

7. Glue remaining fabric to the side edges of the album. See Figure 18.

8. Measure length and width of the inside covers of album. Cut two pieces of light-weight poster board this size. Cut two lining fabric (or decorative paper) pieces ½ inch larger all around than this size. Lay fabric pieces on your work surface with wrong sides up; place poster board pieces on top. Apply glue around all edges of poster board; bring fabric up around poster board and press into glue, mitering corners (fold in from corners first, then sides). See Figure 19.

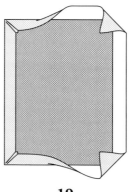

19

Apply glue over the just-glued fabric. Turn over and place the covered poster board, fabric side up, on the inside of the album cover. You may wish to weight down the opened album while the glue dries.

Finishing a Photo Frame

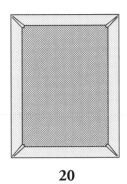

20

Materials
●Heavyweight cardboard, such as 300-pound illustration board
● Fabric (firmly woven cotton or similar)
● Thick white glue
● Scissors
● Pencil
● Felt-tip pen
● Craft knife, utility knife, or single-edged razor blade

Directions (see Figures 20-25)
Follow your project instructions for covering the front of the frame with the cross-stitched fabric. To make the backing and finish the frame, follow the steps below.

1. Using the outer edge of the frame front as a pattern, cut out the cardboard backing. Cut the fabric 1 inch larger all around than the cardboard. Center the cardboard, back side down, over the wrong side of the fabric and glue the corners of the fabric to the cardboard, pulling fabric taut to eliminate wrinkles. Next, glue the sides of the fabric in place. See Figure 20.

2. Cut another piece of fabric ¼ inch smaller all around than the cardboard. Glue this piece to the front side of the cardboard, covering the edges of the previously wrapped fabric. See Figure 21. Both sides of the cardboard are now covered; let dry before proceeding.

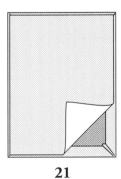

21

3. Cut strips of cardboard ½ inch wide to fit the two side edges and bottom edge of the fabric-covered cardboard. Glue the strips along the edges of the front side of the cardboard, to create a space for your picture. See Figure 22.

22

5. Trace an easel from an existing frame and use as a pattern to cut an easel from leftover cardboard. Score lightly about 1 inch from top edge. Cover both sides of easel with leftover fabric in same manner as back of frame, mitering corners as shown. See Figures 24a and 24b.

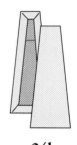

24a   **24b**

4. When both front and back of frame are dry, glue them together, applying glue only to the cardboard strips around the edges. See Figure 23.

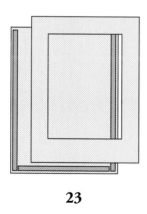

23

Glue the easel to the back of the frame as shown. See Figure 25. You may wish to weight down the frame while it dries. When it is completely dry, insert picture.

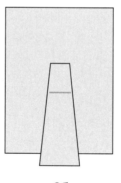

25

Chart Appendix

For your convenience, the large project charts are shown, reduced and assembled, in this section. The grid lines correspond to the heavy grid lines on the symboled stitching charts.

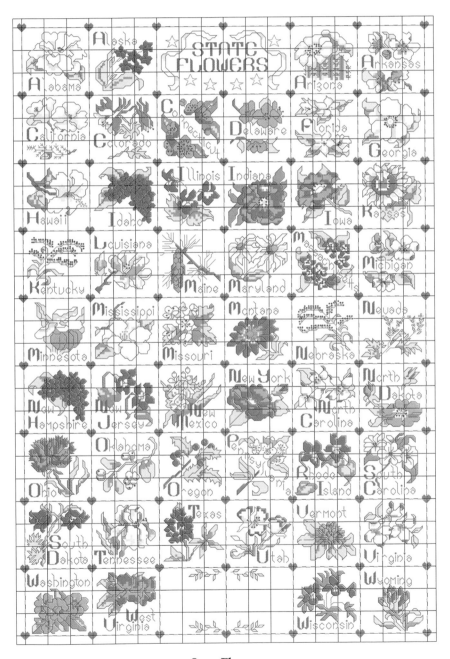

State Flowers

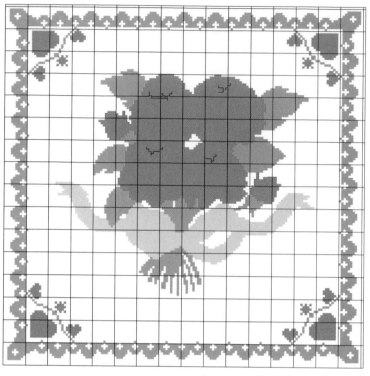

Rose Garden

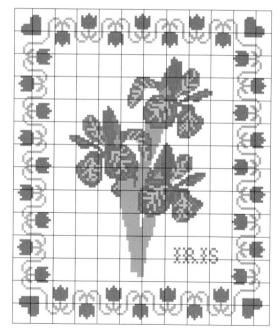

Botanical Flowers

Botanical Flowers

Spring Flowers

Botanical Flowers

Botanical Flowers

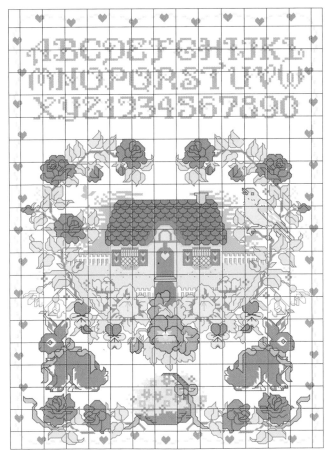

A Child's Garden

Flower Garden

Wildflower Garden

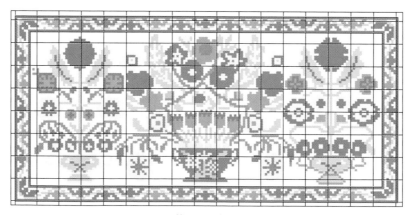

Folk Art Flowers

Wedding Flowers

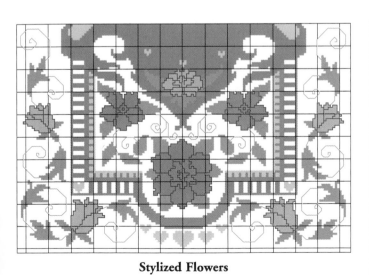

Stylized Flowers

Christmas Flowers

Victorian Valentine

Acknowledgments

It takes a number of people to put together a beautiful book
like this and we would like to give them our thanks.

First, the designers of this collection of glorious projects:

Chapter 1, Spring Flowers;
Barbara Sestok

Chapter 2, A Child's Garden;
Barbara Sestok

Chapter 3, Wildflower Garden;
Judy Chrispens

Chapter 4, Wedding Flowers;
Ursula Michael

Chapter 5, Rose Garden;
Yvonne Beecher

Chapter 6, State Flowers;
Barbara Sestok

Chapter 7, Flower Garden;
Yvonne Beecher

Chapter 8, Stylized Flowers;
Judy Chrispens

Chapter 9, Victorian Valentine;
Mimi Shimmin

Chapter 10, Botanical Flowers;
Yvonne Beecher

Chapter 11, Folk Art Flowers;
Mimi Shimmin

Chapter 12, Christmas Flowers;
Barbara Sestok

We would also like to extend our thanks to the dedicated stitchers who assisted in the completion of the pieces:
Maria Arnold
Susan Chamis
Constance Gerhardt
Rita Jordan
Georgina Simon
Beth Smathers
Jan Woodbury
Catherine Woods

Finding the right setting for photography is another important part of creating a beautiful book. The following homeowners were kind enough to allow us to photograph in their lovely homes and gardens:
Sieglinde Anderson
Ren Chandler
Jean Cohen
Gloria Lonergan
Ellie Schneider

Source List

The project directions in this book call for materials that are widely available in craft stores. If you have difficulty locating specific items, contact the manufacturers or distributors listed below to find sources in your area.

Anchor/Marlitt Floss
Coats & Clark, Inc.
Consumer Service Dept.
P.O. Box 27067
Greenville, SC 29616

Anne Brinkley Designs
available through:
Stitchworks
1502 21st Street NW
Washington, DC 20036
(800) 558-WOOL

Charles Craft
P.O. Box 1049
Laurinburg, NC 28353
(800) 346-4721

Jeanette Crews Designs
4 Killian Hill Road
Lilburn, GA 30247
(800) 241-1962

Dharma Trading Co.
P.O. Box 150916
San Rafael, CA 94915
(800) 542-5227

Prym Dritz
(Fray Check™)
P.O. Box 5028
Spartanburg, SC 29304

DMC--to order floss,
contact:
Herrschners Inc.
2800 Hoover Road
Stevens Point, WI 54481
(800) 441-0838

Kreinik Manufacture
P.O. Box 1966
Parkersburg, WV 26102
(800) 624-1928

Mill Hill Glass Beads
Gay Bowles Sales
P.O. Box 1060
Janesville, WI 53547
(800) 447-1332

Offray Ribbons
Route 24
Chester, NJ 07930

Pat and Pam
P.O. Box 5008
Lubbock, TX 79408
(506) 792-0844

Sudberry House
Box 895
Old Lyme, CT 06371
(203) 739-6951

Wichelt Imports
Route 1, Highway 35
Stoddard, WI 54658

Yarn Tree Designs
P.O. Box 724
Ames, IA 50010
(515) 232-3121

Zweigart--to order fabric,
contact:
Rosemary Drysdale
80 Long Lane
East Hampton, NY 11937
(516) 324-1705

Index

Page numbers in italics indicate photographs.